THE FIRST GHETTO

OR VENETIAN EXEMPLARINESS

Alice Becker-Ho
Translated by John McHale

1968 Press

First published in English 2022 by 1968 Press

Le premier ghetto, ou l'exemplarité vénitienne by Alice Becker-Ho was first published in French by Riveneuve éditions, Paris, 2014

ISBN: 978-1-9196019-2-2 (pbk & ebk)

Printed by Clays Ltd., Bungay

1968 Press

London

To the Serenissima

Contents

Translator's Preface:
Ghettoblast

Rarely has there been such a level of consensus on the one hand about what a term denotes and on the other, a free-for-all concerning not only the word's origin but what it refers to and what it actually means. As the author here makes clear, the consensus in this case revolves around an overarching notion of imprisonment reflected in the innumerable, generally negative or lawless contexts in which the term ghetto takes pride of place. Indeed, a series of clashes can be said to have characterized attempts down through the centuries by ghetto-ologists, historians, philologists, etymologists and linguists in their sometimes convoluted quest to establish the term's origin. When not reaching for metal foundries, etymologies have generally run the gamut from the plausible to the downright preposterous.

As an extremely welcome foray into this long-standing muddle, the present work situates the Venice ghetto firmly within its early sixteenth-century surroundings as depicted cartographically in Jacopo de' Barbari's map of 1500 and administratively in the Venetian Council's 1516 decree: in la Corte de case che sono in Geto apresso san hieronymo [in the court of houses that are in the Ghetto below (the church) of Saint Jerome], drawing a line in the process, as the reader will see, from the fondaci [dei Tedeschi, dei Turchi] to a Venetian-language diminutive, i. e. fóntego, fonteghéto.

Careful consideration of European mercantile history alongside other key historical and philological factors thus combine in *The First Ghetto; or, Venetian Exemplariness* with a detailed consideration of Venice's strategic importance as imperial trading hub, maritime crossroads and point of East-West convergence to clear up a slew of misunderstandings concerning a particularly egregious case of use and abuse.

In the course of a work that offers a significant new insight into a forensically memorialized city, the solution to what has long remained a linguistic puzzle touches on the very essence of the mechanisms of global finance, civic exchange and early modern urban development.

It is very much to be hoped that the present findings will help to provide a more rounded picture and foster a more nuanced understanding of a term which has so often been used to devastatingly incendiary effect, particularly in the English-speaking world.

John McHale

Foreword

"General discussions often produce errors and fallacies
… truth always accompanies and follows particularity
and distinction".
Rabbi Simone Luzzato of Venice, *Discourse on the
Condition of the Jews, Especially in Venice* (1638)

An enormous quantity of ink has been spilled
about Venice and its *Ghetto* without the original meaning
of the latter word ever being properly determined.

The only thing acknowledged with any certainty
is that the term *ghetto* first made its official appearance
in 1516, the date when, following lengthy negotiations
based on the system of the *Condotta* [ruling],* the City
of Doges granted the Jews a renewable charter author-
izing them to create a system of loans accompanied by a
guaranteed right of abode. At that time *Ghetto* — a term
still in use today — denoted the district situated in the
sestiere [sixth] of Cannaregio where the Jews had leave

---

* *Term from Roman law denoting a leasing or renting agreement
whereby the possession of a piece of land or property is relinquished for
a certain amount of time and in return for payment.*

to reside. As time went on, the term came gradually to replace what had previously been known as "The Jewish Quarter", "Jew's Row", "Jewry", etc. everywhere around the world that city-dwelling Jewish communities had established themselves.

Even though the term has gained universal currency, there is still uncertainty among historians about its origin and actual meaning. One hypothesis after the other has been put forward but none has provided the key to what appears to be a genuine mystery. Out of all those that have surfaced to date, some lack all historical or basic common sense, while others flout the most elementary rules of linguistics. However, they have all resorted, for want of anything better, to notoriously hoary stereotypes. Among the most persistent of those regarding the institution of the Ghetto is the one having the negative connotation of imprisonment. In order to support this particular assertion, the conventional approach has comprised an all-out effort to tailor reality to this idea, resorting to any old trumped-up etymology for the purpose. Thus do we come full circle.

Current usage of the term *ghetto* tends nevertheless to denote either some affinity grouping along, say, social and cultural lines (as in *intellectual ghetto*) or some segregated, specifically outcast entity (as in *black ghetto*). It should, however, be noted that barely a hundred years ago *ghetto* was not, for all that, the term chosen to denote particular districts of some American urban centres home to immigrant populations, districts that instead went by the names of *Chinatown*, *Little Italy*, or *Little Russia*. Yet today, as defined by the *Encyclopaedia Universalis*, *ghetto* is the blanket term for "a topological residential development allotted, so to speak, to an underprivileged minority (such as the black population, especially in the United States)".

To return to Venice, what was the meaning of the word *ghetto*? Where did it come from? To what did it refer? At what historical juncture, in what context and for what reasons did it arise? In what way, if any, was the ghetto an exception or a peculiarly Venetian phenomenon? Did it have antecedents and if so, where, when and of what kind? How, if at all, did it differ from the early Jewish communities located in an urban setting? How was it perceived elsewhere at the time? What do the terms foreigner and citizen actually mean and how do they differ? What part has been played at various points by religion, trade, the State, wars, popular uprisings, expulsions, etc?

The foregoing questions need to be tackled by arguing on the basis of not only historical but also linguistic evidence before an open-minded foray can be made into the kind of *Corte sconta** symbolized in such poetic fashion by the Ghetto of Venice, and a few other unsuspected *arcana* unearthed along the way.

In terms of method, as with my previous research on the origins of slang, where there is nothing particularly original about what I have had to say, I have seen fit "to straightforwardly present original quotations whose authors will thereby be accessible to every reader".**

---

* *Corte sconta, or "secret courtyard of Arcana" as imagined by Hugo Pratt in his Fable of Venice.*
** *Preface to the second French edition in Alice Becker-Ho, The Princes of Jargon: A Neglected Factor at the Origins of Dangerous-Class Slang (Edwin Mellen Press, NY, 2004).*

The Foundations of the City

"What happened rather with the rise of cities was that many functions that had theretofore been scattered and unorganized were brought together within a limited area, and the components of the community were kept in a state of dynamic tension and interaction."
Lewis Mumford, *The City In History*

"A city that is of one man only is no city."
Sophocles, *Antigone*

In the work that he devoted to the rise and development of the city, Lewis Mumford portrayed Venice as having been a paragon of success in terms of town planning and socio-political organization. On the basis of what criteria though should Venice be regarded as having the qualities that made it a city *par excellence* and above all else, what exactly is a city?

Owing to the fact that the subject has been comprehensively analysed by numerous historians, there will be no need here to dwell on the long period leading up to the emergence of cities worthy of the name. A brief summary may nevertheless be given of the main portents of this emergence.

a) The substratum

Of all the determining factors, according to Fustel de Coulanges, it was the crucial role of *worship* that forged the original bond: "just as a domestic altar held the members of a family grouped around it, so the city was a collective group of those who had the same protecting deities, and who performed the religious ceremony at the same altar ... if we wished to give an exact definition of a citizen, we should say that it was a man who had the religion of the city".[1]

From the point of view of topography, everybody agrees that the location and function of the *citadel* or "little city" heralded the overturning of the old way of life. Transformed into an impregnable fortress, this sacred spot would be protected by a wall that was itself sacred and therefore impregnable, before coming to encompass the entire city which would in turn enjoy the same privilege of impregnability. On this score, Mumford points out that "deprived of such sacred powers, the ancient city could have been only a heap of baked mud or stones, formless, purposeless, meaningless."[2]

Thus in Greece the *polis* — etymologically the citadel — originally denoted the Acropolis which means the highest point of the town. Consequently, "as the citadel and its immediate surroundings became the religious and political centre, the word gradually took on the meaning of 'town' and ... finally designated the city state. ... The *polis*, perched on a rocky height and surrounded with ramparts, attracted by its military strength the population, who felt safe within its walls or at the foot of the stronghold. Thus were born the first urban agglomerations, which were able to command more extensive groups than the old associations of villages"[3] as Auguste Jardé explains.

For his part, Mumford stresses the fact that in the fortified city, "the wall itself was worth a whole army", supporting this assertion with particular reference to the Spartans whose ruling classes "living in open villages and declining to take refuge behind walls ... had to remain savagely alert and threatening under arms at all times, lest they be overthrown by the enslaved helots".[4] "In Sparta the city was not a town but a camp."[5]

Given that the main feature of urban space was the outer wall, Venice, *which had no such thing*, would have to compensate for this absence in other ways.

Among the other components of village organization that would come to feature in a more complex civic structure were above all the house, altar, well, street, square and market. As in the technical field, the city was indebted to the village. According to Mumford, "out of it came, directly or by elaboration, the granary, the bank, the arsenal, the library, the store" who adds that in the village Council of Elders lay "the beginnings of organized morality, government, law and justice."[6] Henceforth the former local chief would become the guardian of sacred sites and be promoted in turn to the office of king, priest, judge, warlord and ruler of the city prior to giving way to the aristocracy and generally ending up with only a religious remit. This also goes for Bernard Lewis's description of

3

pre-Islamic Mecca where "the union of the clans forming the town was outwardly expressed by a collection
of stones in one central shrine with a common symbol.
The cube-shaped building known as the Ka'ba was such
a symbol of unity in Mecca, where a council known as
the *Mala'*, drawn from the Majlises of the clans, replaced
the simple tribal Majlis. Here the conditional and con-
sensual character of sheikhly authority was weakened
and to some extent supplanted by a kind of oligarchy of
ruling families."[7]

In conclusion, it should be borne in mind that
the village, with its circumscribed rituals and objectives could not, by population growth alone, have become a city. As Mumford explains, this was because "it
is not the numbers of people in a limited area alone,
but the number that can be brought under unified control to form a highly differentiated community, serving
purposes that transcend nurture ... Out of these functions and processes arises a higher capacity for coop-
eration, and a widening of the area of communication
and emotional communion, ... the city broke down the
parsimonious self-sufficiency and dreamy narcissism
of village culture."[8]

This revolution would come, moreover, to leave
its mark on language: "*Villa* entered the French language to give *ville* [town, city], thereby underlining the
town-countryside relationship" according to Georges Jehel who adds that "elsewhere, especially in Italy, the term
civitas with its legal and administrative connotations,
gained currency",[9] "*civitas*, meaning literally the *cives*,
"fellow citizens" as a whole."[10] Added to which, for the
purpose of describing the city, the term *urbs* in the sense
of an area marked by boundaries, is the antithesis of *orbs*
denoting everything outside it. To sum up in Mumford's
words: "the three most essential functions of the city

[are] cultural storage, dissemination and interchange, and creative addition."[11]

b) Citizen and foreigner

For the ancient Greeks, mankind fell originally into two distinct groups: the Greek world and the barbarian, i.e. non-Greek, world in which they would lump civilizations as accomplished as ancient Egypt and Persia. Shaping this world view was the community of language which alone granted access to the community of worship, a prerequisite for obtaining the right of citizenship. The foreigner who is ineligible by definition cannot therefore hope to enjoy this right. As long as no new religions were introduced without its permission, Athens, which always prided itself on the welcome it afforded to strangers, could allow both passing foreigners and resident *Metics* to practise their own religion with no question of ever granting them famed *full civic rights*. Indeed, as Auguste Jardé points out, "in every period, we see foreigners living among citizens. From the very beginning, the stranger, like the poor man and the suppliant, was under the protection of the gods, and of Zeus in particular."[12]

Only citizens enjoyed the full range of political rights and were thus sole participants in public life. As Gustave Glotz makes clear: "the Athenians, proud as they were of being free citizens, were perhaps still prouder of being equal citizens ... equal before the law";[13] furthermore, according to Jardé, "the law, whether the city was an aristocracy or a democracy, was held to be the expression of the general will. It was because the laws of the city guaranteed rights to him that the citizen recognized that he had duties towards it. The barbarian, on the contrary, was a subject, obeying a master."[14]

In order to gain admittance to the city, the stranger passing through it had to take advantage of the special protection of a citizen whom he had to have as a host (the *prostate*), and who afforded him "not only a bed, a place at the fire, and often board as well, but help and protection of every kind. At the beginning hospitality filled the place of international law. There was, moreover, a natural reason for it in the absence of any establishment open to travellers."[15]

Thus thanks to the growing ease of communications fostering trade and industry, towns in the course of their development increasingly opened themselves up to a variegated mass of foreigners, travellers, merchants, refugees and slaves, all of whom in one way or another would contribute to urban transformation and wealth.

Alongside transient foreigners, there would be those henceforth electing to set up home. A class of domiciled foreigners would spring up called Metics.*

"The Metic was not a citizen, but he came within the organization of the city. He retained certain disabilities from his previous condition", as Jardé points out. "He paid the Metic tax, a direct poll-tax, which was, however, very light. Like other foreigners, he paid market dues from which citizens were exempt."[16] Just as in Rome, he was not permitted to own any land since such ownership remained the mark of the citizen.

In return for services rendered, foreigners could, however, see their condition improved by individual and unilateral measures such as

---

* *Metic, ex the Greek prefix meta [change] and oikos [house].*

the right to acquire property, land, an exemption from taxes, etc.

On the other hand in Rome, as Fustel de Coulanges reminds us, "to be enabled to engage in trade, to make contracts, to enjoy his property securely, to have the benefits of the laws of the city to protect him, the foreigner must become the client of a citizen."[17]

In his analysis, Pierre Roussel has this to say: "Although banned from government and property ownership, the Metics led an existence that was not only bearable but in many ways contented and enviable. As far as the law and taxes were concerned, Metics were on a more or less equal footing with citizens; they had their own religious and special shrines, yet took part in some national celebrations."[18] Moreover, those foreigners already domiciled for some time would be regarded as fully-fledged citizens at liberty to engage in any industrial and commercial activity. According to Jardé's description, "the Metic would find work alongside the citizen, either as a craftsman, or, still better, as a trader, from the small retailer to the great merchant who freighted whole fleets and invested his capital in every trading centre in the Hellenic Mediterranean."[19] And, "apart from the craftsmen, who might be either citizens of low degree, free foreigners, or slaves, the expanding mercantile facilities of the agora were in the hand of the Metics",[20] as indeed were large property fortunes whereby a monopoly was also had on the trade in money.

Originally mere moneychangers in the agora at the stall or bench* on which they counted the money, the Metics would gradually come to broaden their activities.

---

* Related to bank [cf. French banque, ex Lombard panka and its corollary banqueroute [bankrupt] ex Italian banca rotta]. The Old French word banchage denoted the duty paid on the bench displaying the merchant's wares.

These ranged from advances to city states or individuals, mortgage loans, bills of exchange, etc. to "adventure capital loans" granted to a ship owner or merchant pledging a vessel or cargo as security. "The entire running of major industrial concerns was in Metic rather than Athenian hands ... . They dominated the spinning and weaving mills, the fur trade, the building, metal working and ceramic industries ... . Their sailing vessels, capital input and labour ... were key to the brilliance and ingenuity of Athenian industry and trade."[21] Mumford remarks on this score that "the Greek contempt for trade was self-defeating: the good faith and reciprocity needed in all forms of long-distance commerce, dependent upon credit, never spread from business to politics" comparing "the foreign trader in the fifth-century Greek economy" with the part played by "the Jew in the Christian economy of the medieval town: he was needed but not wanted."[22]

Equally worthy of note is the emergence of confraternities in commercial towns, "especially in the ports and their suburbs where the Metics attracted unceasingly new influxes of strangers." Gustave Glotz is further of the view that" as freedom of association was unrestricted, groupings by nationalities, by professions, by religions especially, were very easily made."[23] Hence the universal marker of toponymy gives us: "'Harley Street', 'Madison Avenue', 'State Street' ... shorthand expressions not just for occupations, but for a whole way of life that they embody. Rome and Antioch, yes, probably Nineveh and Ur, had their equivalents",[24] but there occurs a shorthand expression too for an established foreign nation such as the one in Venice.

The Cosmopolitan City

"This cosmopolitan ideal was realised in the great commercial cities which welcomed foreigners, and conferred full civic rights very freely."
Jean Hatzfeld, *History of Ancient Greece*

It was doubtless "the unification of the Greek world under Alexander and that of the Mediterranean world under Rome", according to Ferdinand Lot, which "influenced to a very great extent the expansion of Mediterranean commerce."[1]

Up to that point, Greek trade proper had dominated the Mediterranean. For the time being, the port of Piraeus would continue to function as the world's entrepôt from where every sea route ferried goods towards the ports of Asia Minor, Egypt, Italy, Sicily, and even Western lands. However, as trade turned increasingly eastward, Greek towns would begin to decline and see their inhabitants emigrate in ever larger numbers, either towards the long-established cities of Asia Minor or to more recently established towns.

Then it was "through markets and warehouses established along the coasts", as Pierre Roussel points out, "that Athenian Hellenism gained a foothold throughout ... semi-barbarian lands and that the whole of Mediterranean Asia and Egypt came to be permeated by Hellenism."[2]

Within such a context, differences in origin will tend to dissolve, engendering a cosmopolitan ideal devoid of "all distinguishing features and local roots in order to cater to the needs of the almost uniform urban class populating the main towns throughout the Greco-Macedonian kingdoms."[3]

A common language (the *koinè*) would even emerge, used by Greeks "steeped in dialects" and "multilingual" foreigners, and which would become the language of Hellenized towns. In Mumford's view, "the Hellenistic city ... was above all an 'emporium'."[4]

Among the models of their kind, the following examples may be cited:

a) Constantinople

Founded towards 658 BCE on the banks of the Bosphorus, the former Byzantium, which had once been among the great maritime powers, was plundered and razed to the ground by the Roman legions of Septimus Severus.

After his conversion to Christianity, the Emperor Constantine (280/288-337 CE) decided to make Byzantium his capital city. On the 11th May 330 it was renamed *Roma Nova*. Magnificently rebuilt, it then re-emerged as Constantinople, marking the beginning of the Byzantine Empire.

Admirably situated "where Europe meets Asia ... Constantinople formed a natural hub around which the Eastern world clustered."[5] A prized possession, the reign of Theodosius II (408-450 CE) saw the building of a powerful system of ramparts that proved so effective in defending Constantinople down through the centuries. Added to which Justinian (518-610 CE) ordered the construction of a continuous line of fortresses along every border. As a result, the attack on Constantinople by the Muslims, who were nevertheless the subsequent conquerors of most of the Eastern world, failed to take it.

"Even under Roman rule, Hellenism had remained vibrant and strong throughout the Greek Orient"[6] asserts Charles Diehl. And in the seventh century, the title of "basileus" would be given to every Byzantine emperor, while Greek became the official language and low Greek that spoken by the bulk of the population. Thus Greek gave "the appearance of being the national language"[7] in a cosmopolitan empire comprising twenty different nationalities. This was also the moment when orthodoxy "merged in Byzantium with nationality."[8]

From 867 to 1025, the Byzantine Empire experienced one and a half centuries of incredible splendour. Moreover, in the tenth century the Greek empire stretched from the Danube to Syria, from the shores of Italy to the plateaux of Armenia. "By virtue of its merchants, the power of its navy, the commercial hubs that its ports and great markets provided, Byzantium cornered the entire wealth of the planet"[9] is Charles Diehl's analysis. Venice, wholly Greek in origin and conduct, was then the most loyal and docile of the Empire's vassals.

Alvise Zorzi notes that "in March 992, the Byzantine emperors Basil and Constantine promulgated a

11

chrysobull [golden edict] that guaranteed the Venetian merchants a distinct advantage over their Amalfitan, Apulian Lombard and Jewish competitors in exchange for military aid against the Arabs"[10] adding that "in 1082, in return for their participation in the campaign against the Guiscard Normans who landed in Epirus, a new "chrysobull" guaranteed the Venetians "a raft of privileges specifically tailored to ensure the enrichment of Venice ... Its trade in the Byzantine world was permanently exempted from taxes while the commercial hubs of the Mediterranean Levant, from Laodicea to Antioch in Syria ... and many other cities, were opening up to it."[11] As Zorzi makes clear, "In Constantinople itself, an entire district along the Golden Horn had been conceded to the Venetians where they already had their church, their bath house and their ovens."[12] Soon however in Élisabeth Crouzet-Pavan's summation, "everywhere in the Eastern Mediterranean, and even in Byzantine areas, the Venetians saw their former preponderance challenged. First, the chrysobull of 1111 granted to the Pisans deprived the Venetians of their quasi-monopoly; next, in 1118 the new emperor, John II Comnenus, refused to confirm the privileges that had been accorded to Venice in 1082."[13] The crucial turning point for Byzantium came with the Crusades.

On the pretext of freeing the Holy Places occupied by infidels, many a feudal noble wished to carve out a few principalities as their personal fiefdoms. From 1118 to 1130, the Venetian fleet had come to the Crusaders' aid, winning the Battle of Ascalon and, by taking Tyre from the Muslims, winning "for the Crusaders undisputed control of the sea for a generation"[14] as Frederic C. Lane notes. The antagonism between Greeks and Venetians intensified. Despite the Emperor Manuel I Comnenus' need for the Venetians and the tokens of friendship that he lavished on them, he set about the arrest in 1171 of every Venetian in the Empire and the confiscation of their possessions.

While the resourceful Doge Ziani was managing to renew trading privileges, Manuel Comnenus, for his part, continued to grant corresponding ones to rivals.

In 1187, the Fourth Crusade was decided upon, Saladin's victories having practically obliterated all but a few coastal towns in the kingdom of Jerusalem. Suspecting it of sealing a pact with Saladin, Venice arranged to have this Crusade diverted to Constantinople.

F. C. Lane recounts that in April 1204, the capture of Constantinople saw "three days of murder, rapine, rape and sacrilege. ... The four bronze horses which had once stood on top of a triumphal arch in Rome, then over the racing stadium in Constantinople, ... now stand in front of San Marco."[15]

By then "the sick man of Europe", the Empire in its entirety fell into Crusaders' hands, culminating in the coronation on the 16th May 1204 of Count Baldwin of Flanders as Roman Emperor.

As for the Venetians, Jean Longnon recounts that "with the exception of one whole quayside district by the Golden Horn, they recovered all their former imperial possessions, together with complete freedom of movement and leave to freight all goods exempt from duty."[16] Scion of the most eminent Venetian families, the *baile* [bailiff] not only administered the city district given over to the Venetians but assumed stewardship of Eastern Mediterranean and Black sea concerns.

In Freddy Thiriet's view, "Venice was the main beneficiary"[17] of the 1204 expedition, and "Constantinople became a second Venice, tolerance being the only thing granted to merchants from other cities: three-eighths of the city, together with the church of Santa Sophia were reserved for Venetians clustered around their podestà, a bona fide viceroy or rather vice-doge of Romania ... and the doge of Venice now went by the name of "Lord of One Quarter and One Half [of a Quarter] of the Empire of Romania"."[18]

However, in 1261, Michael VIII Paleologue sought to restore the Byzantine Empire with help from the Genoese to whom he promised to grant all the trade and tax privileges enjoyed by the Venetians once the latter were driven from Constantinople. Even though the city wasted little time in resuming relations with Byzantium, the Latin Empire of Romania's days were numbered. "Indeed, the West lost interest in the Byzantine Empire, or only sought to take advantage of its poverty in order to keep a religious, political and economic grip on it ... . Visits to Italy, France and England in 1369, 1402 and 1439 by John V, Manuel II and John VIII respectively for the purpose of obtaining aid were all to no avail: courteous welcomes and fine promises were all that these rulers came away with. And when Mehmet II decided to put an end to the Greek Empire, an exhausted and forlorn Byzantium was simply left to fade away"[19] as Charles Diehl concluded bitterly.

b) Alexandria

"All of Alexandria was the wondrous city and all the others were mere villages in comparison"[20] is how Pierre Roussel puts it. Founded by Alexander the Great in 331 BCE, the city of Alexandria in lower Egypt was originally no more than a fishing village, albeit one equidistant from Greece, Asia Minor and Syria. Ptolemy I, a former general under Alexander, was bequeathed Egypt and made Alexandria its capital. In Bernard Lewis's assessment, "The Ptolemies of Egypt sent ships through the Red Sea, exploring the Arabian coasts and the trade-routes to India. Their successors in the Near East retained that interest."[21] Abram Leon pointed out that "the situation which the Jews had acquired for themselves in the Hellenistic epoch appears to have undergone no fundamental transformation after the Roman conquest ... the role of the Jews at Alexandria was so important that a Jew, Tiberius Julius Alexander, was appointed Roman governor of this city."[22]

"In 642, Alexandria fell into Arab hands, whereupon Rome noticed that large numbers of the populations conquered by the Mahometans quickly adopted the new religion."[23]

The legend that has it that two Venetian merchants brought the remains of the evangelist Saint Mark from Alexandria is the basis for the founding myth of Venice, whence the consecration in 832 of the Basilica of Saint Mark.

A cosmopolitan city *par excellence* where Greeks, Egyptians, Jews and Romans mixed, Alexandria thereafter remained the hub of Mediterranean trade with Arabia and India throughout the Middle Ages, despite the political and spiritual decline that followed the Arab conquest. The thirteenth century would, however, witness the installation of a new Mameluk* regime that governed Egypt and Syria until the arrival of the Ottomans in 1517. The Mameluk sultans profited from the key positions they held by encouraging and safeguarding harbour trade

---

* *Military ruling elite originally purchased as slaves, then trained and brought up in Egypt.*

whilst levying heavy duties that would for a time ensure their prosperity. Of paramount importance for Venice, "which drew its life from maritime trade ... were the acquisition of trading concessions, access to markets and the safety of its trade routes",[24] as Jean-Claude Hocquet points out.

The real decline came only later, after the Portuguese first threw down the gauntlet by opening a new route around the Cape of Good Hope, a move that would inevitably open up competition with the Mediterranean market especially once the great scramble westward in aid of the newly constituted European powers had begun.

However, long before they were cut off from their original supply sources — whether spices from Asia, cotton fabrics and manufactured goods from Syria, or gold from Africa — Venetians were reliably solvent customers who were rewarded with trading privileges and who "held a predominant position among the Western buyers"[25] as Frederic C. Lane observes, going on to say, moreover, that "they had two large and impressive warehouse-palaces, which were among the handsomest structures in Alexandria; the Genoese had only one; the Catalans and French had much smaller establishments."[26]

"In the Latin and Muslim East" explains Michel Balard, "the term of Arabic origin *al-funduq (-fondok or fendenq)* denoted "a generally square-shaped building formed of two or three storeys housing merchants, a ground floor serving as a warehouse and an inner courtyard where goods were unwrapped and exchanged. Reserved for businessmen foreign to the country or city."[27] Anne Raulin has established that "the word really caught on all around the Mediterranean, in Venice, Genoa and

Naples under the same name of *fondaco*,* albeit in various forms — quarters or premises belonging to merchants' families and cropping up in Spanish as *alhondiga* meaning corn exchange, in Portuguese as *alfândega* meaning customs or customs house."[28] In French there existed *fondouck* and *fonde*: "They set fire to the market [*fonde*] where all the merchandise was and all goods sold by weight";[29] and French *fundique, fondique* or *fondic*:** "Fondics are warehouses for storing commodities brought from the Indies and Persia via Aleppo … they also house merchants"[30] is the example cited in Littré.***

To return to Alexandria, Jean-Claude Hocquet points out that "in the great Egyptian port, these foreigners were obliged to reside and conduct their business within the *fondouk* owned and maintained by the local authorities. The [Venetian] Commune that acquired a church and a bath house located outside the *fondouk* prior to 1238 was represented by a consul who obtained from the authorities the right to refuse accommodation to non-Venetians."[31]

These advantages were, however, offset by certain inconveniences. Thus, "like other Christians, the Venetians were forbidden to go outside their compound during the hours of prayer on the Moslem holy day of Friday, and they were locked in at night",[32] as Frederic C. Lane explains. Although nominally under the protection of their consuls, a greater, if less frequent, inconvenience occurred whenever "the resident Venetian merchants, who in good times lived luxuriously in their palace compound, were now and then locked up, beaten

---

* Cf. *fondego, fundaco, funduca, fondaco* in English (*Translator's note*).
** Cf. *funduck, fonduk, fondak* in English (*Translator's note*).
*** Émile Littré, *Dictionnaire de la langue française* (*Translator's note*).

till they bled, and threatened with death".[33] Lane adds, pointing out that "what was surest to arouse the wrath of the soldan was to hear that some of his subjects, Moslem travelling merchants, had been seized at sea and sold into slavery."[34] Wherever this had proven to be the case and as a mark of good faith, Venice showed its resolve by executing the culprits. In exchange for which, against its offers of substantial compensation, it got the sultan not only to free those of its subjects captured in retaliation but even better, was enabled to negotiate new commercial privileges in its own favour.

"To be sure", according to Frederic C. Lane's analysis, "Venetian letters and chronicles repeatedly complain of the greed and savagery of the Mamluks, but that may only prove how ancient is the practice of businessmen who have to deal with government officials of complaining violently about how they are being squeezed, even if their profits are good",[35] drawing attention also to the fact that the Venetians made "lots of money out of the Egyptian spice trade."[36]

c) Trading posts and other ports of call

"From the Ionian islands to Corinth and Thessalonica, from Crete to Paphos, from Smyrna to Byzantium, there was no commercial hub in the Eastern Mediterranean where Venetians did not encounter residents in the shape of their fellow countrymen",[37] or, as Paul Morand put it, "in every Port of the Levant, the world came up against Venetian monopolies as high as aftercastles."[38]

Spread strategically all along the shores of the Mediterranean, these Ports [French *Échelles*] formed a veritable colonial empire based on strong family ties with the home city. "To the Venetians", writes Alvise Zorzi, "Saint Jean d'Acre was home."[39] Jean-Claude Hocquet attests to the fact that "overlooking the port, the Venetian quarter had its own *fondaco* with the Commune of Venice boasting a square surrounded by a comprehensive residential, commercial and trading development which it offered on short-term lets to merchants or pilgrims while long-term residents were charged more moderate rents. Goods reached the *fondaco* after clearing the port and gate-side Royal Custom House, the property of the King of Jerusalem ... The bitter rivalry between the three Latin nations of Venice, Pisa and Genoa prompted the Venetians to surround their neighbourhood with high walls and towers."[40]

Philippe Braunstein and Robert Delort are furthermore of the view that "the merchant quarters of Egypt, Syria and the Black Sea were modelled or remodelled on those of Constantinople",[41] while F. C. Lane adds that "all departures and ports of call were determined by the capitanio [admiral] according to the instructions from the doge and various Councils."[42]

Similar considerations apply to Crete, a crucially important base for La Serenissima which, according to Christian Bec, "populated the island in successive waves with some 10,000 settlers from the home city's six sestieri, spreading them its length and breadth along Venetian administrative lines."[43] "*Sestieri* that bore the names of Venetian districts: San Marco, Castello, Cannaregio, Santa Croce, San Polo, Dorsoduro and in which", Alvise Zorzi rounds off, "the island's infrastructure faithfully mirrored that of the home city."[44]

Of equal strategic importance for the permanently disputed control of sea routes between the two great rivals Genoa and Venice were other maritime possessions such as Modon and Coron (nicknamed "the two eyes of the Republic"), together with Zara, Ragusa, Durazzo, Corfu, Negroponte and Tana.

Thus in Frederic C. Lane's estimation, "in spite of periods of weakness, Venice had maintained the essential of her economic position, namely, being a go-between in the commercial relations of East and West",[45] moreover "Venice at the beginning of the fifteenth century was still basically a maritime republic looking seaward and eastward."[46] However, "political changes within the Mediterranean, as well as developments across the oceans, adversely affected Venetian trade in a number of ways, most of them connected more or less directly with the growth of the Ottoman Empire."[47]

"This marked the emergence of that concerted two hundred and fifty year long sibling rivalry so characteristic of the Mediterranean world right up to the beginning of the eighteenth century ... Concerned for its own survival, La Serenissima came swiftly to terms with the inescapable reality of an omnipotent Ottoman presence. As it turned out, the latter ... would do more to facilitate than to harm Venetian trade"[48] is Alvise Zorzi's conclusion.

The Jewish Community: Exile to Exile

"The Lord exiled Israel among the nations so that proselytes might swell their ranks."
Rabbi Eleazar, *Tractate Pesachim*

"The law of the land is the law."
Talmudic maxim

In the course of his disturbing study on the historical origins of the Jews, Shlomo Sand refers to Chaim Mi-
likowsky, professor at the religious university of Bar-Ilan
who proved "that in the second and third centuries CE
the term *galut* [exile] was used in the sense of political
subjugation rather than deportation, and the two meanings were not necessarily connected."[1] Using rabbinical
sources, he confirms this by demonstrating that the only
exile dating from the sixth century BCE referred to was
the Babylonian one. "Perhaps, following the destruction
of the Second Temple, this gave rise to the narrative linking the fall with renewed exile as an echo of an ancient

event";[2] only later on, "with the triumph of Christianity in the early fourth century CE when it became the religion of the empire, [did] Jewish believers in other parts of the world also begin to adopt the notion of exile as divine punishment."[3] Indeed the same sentiment underpins the following observation by Simon Schwarzfuchs: "They would be more inclined than others to move into cities or new markets ... untroubled by the memory of any lost nearby or far-off homeland ... For them, the Jerusalem of their hopes and dreams had ceased to be earthly and became instead the heavenly object of their prayers."[4] For his part, Leon Poliakov mentions that "in the case of the Spanish Jews, who were deeply rooted in the Iberian peninsula, G[ershom] Scholem's research has shown that the idea of the exile became a central thread of Jewish mysticism only *after* the expulsion from Spain; it is known that in the eleventh century Judah Ha-levi, who urged his co-religionists to stay faithful to the promised land, was crying in the wilderness."[5]

Present-day historians place a heavy emphasis on a kind of dispersion accompanied from the outset by a proselytism that only the predominance of the latest revealed religion would curb.

The foregoing discussion has drawn attention to how, following the conquests of Alexander, the Hellenistic era and its cosmopolitan ideals had arisen by creating new urban hubs throughout the Mediterranean basin. With the formation of the Roman Empire over a vast area, this ongoing process would, in Shlomo Sand's view, open "a fresh perspective for the spread of Judaism; at its high point there, Judaism was professed by 7 to 8 percent of all the empire's inhabitants."[6]

a) Settlement and growth

Regarding the term "Jew" touched upon by the former consul Cassius Dio in his "Roman History" (from the origins to 229 CE), the latter asserted that "I do not know how this title [Jews] came to be given to them, but it applies also to all the rest of mankind, although of alien race, who affect their customs."[7] Thus "the first mention of Judaism in Roman documents has to do with conversion",[8] the only explanation for the "substantial presence [of Jewish believers that] existed for a long time before the war of 70 CE" being "the spread of the Jewish religion"[9] which "had nothing to do with any imaginary "mass expulsions" from Judea after the fall of the kingdom and the Bar Kokhba revolt [in 132]."[10]

It is generally accepted that Jews settled in Rome before Christians did and that, as is evidenced from the Roman Jewish catacombs, they constituted the earliest Jewish community in Europe.

"If hostility to the Jews occasionally broke out, it was due mainly to their religious preaching"[11] regarded as a threat despite the tolerance shown by polytheistic Romans towards a practice they sanctioned as *religio licita*. Mommsen makes the point that "Caesar also advanced the interests of the Jews in Alexandria and in Rome by special favours and privileges, and protected in particular their peculiar worship against the Roman as against the Greek local priests",[12] adding that "[Judaism was] a specially privileged member in the Caesarian state."[13]

Consequently in Rome, where "the first comers arrived as allies of the Romans automatically entitled to Roman protection", they were, as Simon Schwarzfuchs relates, "considered fully-fledged citizens. Free men, they could elect domicile throughout the Roman Em-

pire and so established many communities within its
borders."[14] It should be recalled that outside Italy at
the beginning of the third century CE, a period that
saw the spread of Judaism reach its highest point, the
Empire included Slavonic or German lands, Southern
Gaul and Spain.

Simon Schwarzfuchs further remarks that "it is
likely, if not probable, that the Roman legions took Jewish settlers along with them ... although it is undeniable
that groupings took place very early on in the Northern
Alps and in the Danube Valley, far from the Mediterranean basin. From the fourth century CE, Jews were living in
Cologne and in Pannonia."[15] A new wave of emigration
seems to have ensued after the period of large-scale invasions when, in Abram Leon's assessment, "all the peoples
of the Roman Empire were carried away in [Jerusalem's]
fall. Only the Jews have been preserved because they
brought into the barbarian world, which followed upon
the Roman, vestiges of the commercial development
which had characterized the ancient world."[16]

As noted by Simon Schwarzfuchs, "from the ninth
century CE, Jewish immigration to Northern Europe began again with renewed vigour"[17] with the period leading up to the First Crusade in 1096 one of "community
settlement and growth which, despite a large number
of sporadic crises and conflicts, was marked by Jewish integration into Christian society and a burgeoning
economic role, helped by their concentrated presence
in commercial cities across Europe."[18] As Abram Leon
points out, the period was also when "the evolution in
exchange of the medieval economy proved fatal to the
position of Jews in trade."[19] "Trade advances from the
passive to the active stage ... the development of native production makes possible the rapid formation of
a powerful class of native merchants."[20] Consequently,

"the Crusades, which were also an expression of the will of the city merchants to carve a road to the Orient, furnished them with the occasion for violent persecutions and bloody massacres of the Jews. From this period on, the situation of the Jews in the cities of Western Europe is irrevocably compromised."[21]

The twelfth, thirteenth and fourteenth centuries saw usury thrive in all the countries of Europe. Nachum Tim Gidal makes the point that "those who were in debt with interest-bearing loans from Jewish pawnbrokers increasingly tended to be impoverished knights, the poorer townspeople, and above all poor peasants. Not only did the peasants have to pay their tithes to the church, but also pay duty to the lord of the manor and do certain tasks for him."[22] However, "the indebtedness of the nobles to the Jewish usurers contained the germs of bloody conflicts."[23]

Thus, as Marc Bloch showed, "the emergence of a new class, the *bourgeoisie* and the resuscitation of the State after long eclipse, coincided with the time when the most specifically feudal characteristics of Western civilization began to disappear."[24]

Moreover, "the peasants" mistrust of the merchant and the noble's contemptuous haughtiness found a parallel and a justification on the ideological plane in the teaching of the church ... until the latter was forced to give greater consideration to the changing conditions of real life",[25] as Aron J. Gurevich explains. However, in Nachum T. Gidal's view, "several factors accounted for the fact that the Jews largely lost their position in domestic and international trade. One was the decline of feudalism and the associated strengthening of merchants' associations and guilds; another the development of the cities as marketplaces for the transfer of goods. The Jews were moreover pushed out of large-scale finance because this was increasingly dealt with by monasteries and the new municipal trade companies from the fourteenth century onward."[26]

On the other hand, "the royal power was also obliged to have dealings with leading members of the mercantile and entrepreneurial class, as rulers needed financial aid and political support from them."[27] Hence "this contradictory attitude toward the medieval merchant is perfectly displayed in the sermons of the mendicant friars"[28] whose excesses would give rise to the worst effects of the Inquisition. Furthermore, as Gidal notes, "the end of the thirteenth century saw the construction of the Jewish quarter surrounded by walls which was intended for the exclusive occupation of the Jews."[29]

In these circumstances, Sylvie Anne Goldberg contends that "insofar as Jewish settlement kept pace with the process of urban growth in the Middle Ages, it is indissociable from the formation of a structured community."[30]

b) From grouping to community

"According to feudal law predicated on the Roman model, Jews were *servi camerae regis* [serfs of the Royal Chamber] ... who could nonetheless practise their religion and manage their own domestic affairs such as the levying of taxes and the settlement of disputes by the *beth din* or rabbinical court."[31]

It should be pointed out that the term 'serf' which, under the feudal system denoted anyone bound to the soil and divested of all rights over his own person and possessions, cannot be applied to the particular context of Jewry. It would be more accurate to translate *servi* by *servants* in the sense of "whoever is bound to the State, to a prince, etc.", or, as a thirteenth century French religious order styled itself with the name of "Servants [Fr. serfs] of the Holy Mother of God or *Blancs-Manteaux*": in his book *"Jewish Wanderings"*, Riccardo Calimani makes the point that "the condition of glebe serfs, most of whom had few resources and were more ignorant and boxed-in, was worse than that of the Jews",[32] a view supported by Israel Bartal: "the Jewish community was recognized as a separate entity based on the specific nature of its religion and its ethnic origin. The Jews were deemed to be *servi camerae*, i.e. property of the prince who afforded them protection, any violation of which constituted harm to the integrity of the crown. Only a crown representative could sit in judgement on them and their domestic affairs were entirely their own business."[33]

Further confusion would arise from the way the *oremus et pro perfidis Judaeis* [prayer for the Jews] was interpreted. Robert Anchel explains that the words *perfidis Judaeis* should under no circumstances be taken to mean 'perfidious Jews' here but incredulous, non-believing Jews, Jews lacking true faith … . It would be very odd indeed to describe those for whom one is praying as perfidious."[34]

Present in Europe since the tenth century, the Jewish community (Kahal) is defined by Simon Schwarzfuchs as a "self-governing cell within European society."[35] The same author states that "it was, however, only in the thirteenth century, under the influence of Rabbi Meir of Rothenburg … that the crystallization took place. From then on, the basic framework and principal institutions of the Kahal — or Kehilal — were established … No Jew, short of renouncing his own faith, would be able to free himself from them."[36] "The Kahal was triumphant, and, in spite of many difficulties, would remain so until the French Revolution."[37]

In the process of occupying urban space, the zone where Jews "elected to settle was not originally perceived as a zone where foreigners lived but as an enterprise zone, ... a space devoted to "trade of a specialized nature"[38] in Stefano Zaggia's analysis.

Robert Anchel observes that "the question of the geographical distribution of Jews in France at various historical periods ... has received practically zero attention. It is fairly certain that they had been town and country dwellers and that from the end of the thirteenth century they began to move to towns in greater numbers",[39] pointing out however that "at the time of Gregory of Tours ... Syrian merchants and Jews would set out goods for sale in what is now the square before Notre Dame Cathedral and along the bridges spanning both arms of the Seine ... they would also have had storage areas for these goods ... at a time when they were the sole importers into the West of exotic produce, especially spices, that they had brought from the South of France and the Mediterranean East",[40] and that in Paris "Jews lived at a considerably earlier period in rue de la Juiverie situated on the Île de la Cité."[41]

Fernand Braudel remarks that "in the thirteenth century, the Fairs of Champagne were the centre of western commerce ... . The Jews were there too, in the towns and villages of Champagne, some of them concerned in the agricultural life of the region, others artisans, owning fields, vines, real estate or houses which they bought and sold, but for the most part they were already merchants and moneylenders."[42]

Leon Poliakov mentions that "Jews in all the various countries of the Diaspora had always had a habit of clustering together in their own district, sometimes protected by gates and inside padlocks; in other words, they themselves chose if they wanted to live inside or outside the Jewry."[43]

Wolfgang Kaiser states that "insofar as the demarcation of the foreigner seems to be of a piece with the very definition of the western city, a clear spatial demarcation in the shape of the fonduk or *ghetto* only begins to tackle the problem because underpinning it is the notion of an absolute divide between the urban community and the Other."[44] For her part, Sylvie Anne Goldberg notices that "according to the medieval works on law and the statutes themselves, the ways in which Jews socialized took community as their model. This model, which came to be regarded as traditional, consisted primarily of a cluster of families in one place and was formed around living quarters identified closely with the observance of rituals and daily religious worship",[45] pointing out too that "ranging from the best-appointed to the most rudimentary, such conditions wholly depended upon the "privileges" set out in the charters granting right of abode issued by the princes and bishops of those towns where Jews were welcomed and invited to stay."[46]

The Jewish community or congregation (*qehillah*) was often placed in a specific district of the town, sometimes near their protector-lord's castle ... . The secular authorities or the Church acknowledged the head of the community (*parnas*) as the Jews' official representative."[47] Alan Unterman goes on to explain that "orthodox Jews were required to live fairly close to their synagogue so as to be able to walk there on the Sabbath or for religious feasts, traditional Jewish communities are tightly clustered together."[48]

"The willingly assumed community", as Simon Schwarzfuchs shows, "managed to make the best use of its existence in order to create institutions, employ staff and provide the cohesion and discipline that it regarded as indispensable. It was doubtless harsh and exacting but it could also apply itself to rendering all the services expected of it … . The political authorities sought its subservience and its members, who had no wish to see it disappear, did not always manage to submit to its injunctions."[49]

c) Between integration and separation

Abram Leon's finding that before it "became the ideology of the class of landowners who seized absolute power under Constantine … Christianity was originally the ideology of the poor Jewish masses. The first churches were formed around the synagogues".[50] This should be borne in mind, as well as the fact that "only the Jewish communities with a clearly defined commercial character, numerous in Italy, in Gaul, in Germany etc., proved capable of resisting all attempts at assimilation."[51] As a consequence, "in the first half of the Middle Ages … the Jews were considered as being part of the upper classes in society and their juridical position was not perceptibly different from that of the nobility."[52] It is known moreover that "the finance ministers of the kings of the early Middle Ages were often Jews",[53] but that "in those places where Jews abandoned business in order to become real landowners, sooner or later they necessarily also changed their religion … But a Jewish landowner in the Middle Ages could only be an anomaly."[54] In Wolfgang Kaiser's view, "the special moment in the foreigner's lot is the transition from foreigner to bourgeois."[55]

Michael Wex is of the opinion that "Judaism is obsessed with separation, with boundaries",[56] that "*the mitsves* [commandments] act as hedges against this sort of assimilation."[57] "The Jews", he declares, "sought as much independence from the surrounding society as was practicable for people who still needed to make a living and eat."[58] Thus in Simon Schwarzfuchs' exposition, "a town within a town, the community had to cater for its members' needs and come to their defence if necessary",[59] whether tackling the threat posed by "Christian powers" or "some of its own members' unruliness" who "rejected or weakened its essence."[60] "It might be thought", as Béatrice Philippe points out, "that medieval Jewish communities maintained only a conflictual relationship with the authorities",[61] while noting that "contemporary chronicles teem with details that show that in everyday life, Jews and Christians mixed together and were sometimes on the friendliest of terms"[62] and that "given that, by and large, the crowd remained passive in the face of the harassment visited on the Jews, some people were nevertheless conspicuous by the tolerance and consideration they showed them."[63] Similarly in Germany, the integration of Jews "into their surroundings was such that at the first sign of trouble, they nevertheless remained incredulous and passive".[64] While as Gilbert Dahan further points out, "groups on the fringes of the official Crusade … attacked the cities and the Jews, in some cases (in Moers for example) bourgeois helped the Jews, while in others they handed them over to the looters in order to save their own skins. In Speyer, Bishop John managed to protect the Jews and protection was also afforded them in Cologne. Yet the end result was appalling since a dozen communities were virtually wiped out."[65] Dahan notes too that during the Second Crusade in 1146 "the swift and robust intervention of Bernard, abbot of Clairvaux"[66] succeeded in putting a stop to further mayhem. Referring to the earliest charges of ritual murder brought against the Jews initially in England and France and thereafter in thirteenth century Germany, Dahan makes the point that both "the Pope and the Emperor respectively took on their traditional roles of protectors in order to assert the Jews' innocence."[67] Riccardo Calimani mentions that "the bull entitled '*Constitutio pro Judaeis*' set out in formal terms the Church's official attitude to the Jews."[68] For her part, Sylvie Anne Goldberg states that "the transformations affecting the political and religious spheres ... never posed any challenge, however, to Jewish self-jurisdiction."[69] Riccardo Calimani further remarks that "Alexander III had convoked the Third Lateran Council (1179). The Pope, who at that time had a Jewish administrator, Jehiel ben Abraham, ... adopted no new restrictive measures and on the contrary, even issued a message of tolerance: forced baptism was prohibited, Jews should not be mistreated and their religious observances should continue unimpeded."[70]

Gilbert Dahan judges that throughout the fourteenth century, wars, epidemics, religious and political upheavals would give rise to "aggressive impulses [that] came to focus on the Jews ... . Indeed, to all appearances, persecutions had triumphed over any eventual integration. Yet there is no doubt that a more nuanced appraisal is required: no matter how numerous and dramatic events became ... they nonetheless represented glitches in a situation that tended more towards integration."[71]

While all around, "even more efficient as a cause of misery to the people and hostility towards the Church was the venality of many of the episcopal courts",[72] Henry Charles Lea mentions that "one of the main objects in convoking the great Council of Lateran, in 1215, was the correction of the prevailing vices of the clergy"[73] "but on this score as on so many others the numerous canons it adopted [were] in vain."[74]

Simon Schwarzfuchs points out that "at the same time, towards the middle of the thirteenth century, the representatives of the sisterhoods of Worms, Speyer and Mainz adopted the legislative enactments [takkanot] forbidding "every Jew to dress like Christians or wear their hair like them"",[75] specifying that "everything was done to stamp out a certain tendency toward ostentation, regarded as dangerous owing as much to the envy it could arouse among Christians as to a ruinous competition between the members of the community obsessed with appearances."[76]

In fact, "the blows which brought real danger to the hierarchy came from obscure men, labouring among the poor and oppressed",[77] through whom heresy spread, mainly in the South of France where prelates, according to Henry Charles Lea, were "powerless to arrest the progress of the bold heresiarch and imploringly appealed for assistance."[78] In the face of this danger, confronted as they were by the intrigues of pious and greedy princes eager to get their hands on confiscated goods, and regardless of Bernard of Clairvaux's injunction that "faith is to be produced by persuasion, not imposed by force", the popes delegated all power to the preachers. Béatrice Leroy stresses that "the Inquisition proper dates back to the Albigensian heresy which had placed the very existence of the Church in jeopardy. Placed originally under Dominican Order control, it had already demonstrated its zeal."[79] Leroy points out too that "once this problem had been partially solved, the Inquisition attacked the Judaizing heretics and apostates who had returned to Judaism after their conversion. As for declared Jews, they were outside the Church and, short of being guilty of religious meddling or attacks on Christianity, did not fall within its

sphere of activity."[80] For his part, Henry Charles Lea crit-
icizes the inconsistency of "the persecutors of the thirteenth century [who] made one concession to humanity
and common-sense which was fatal to the completeness
of the theory on which they acted. To carry it out ful-
ly, they should have proselyted with the sword among
all non-Christians whom fate threw in their power; but
from this they abstained. Infidels who had never received the faith, such as Jews and Saracens were not to be
compelled to Christianity."[81] In addition, Gilbert Dahan
draws attention to another paradox: "from the Middle
Ages onward, the weight of history has endowed Ashkenazi Judaism with specific features, crucial to which is
the fact that Jews were never expelled from Germany
(on the contrary, communities there welcomed refugees
from England, France and later on from Spain). Crucial
too because, at a time (fourteenth and fifteenth centuries)
when Europe was going through a series of crises and
changes, the Jews were there to crystallize every fear: of
the Other, the unknown, the Devil."[82] Of crucial importance too since it accounts for German Jewish withdraw-
al "into their own traditions, values and a hermeticism
that would surprise sixteenth and seventeenth century
humanist travellers."[83] Yet if "the attitude of the kings
and princes toward the Jews therefore appears somewhat contradictory",[84] for Abram Leon "it is determined
in the last analysis by economic development"[85] and for
whom "religion explains anti-Jewish persecutions like a
sleeping pill explains sleep"[86], further opining that "in
general, the period of medieval capitalism was that of
the most violent Jewish persecutions"[87] since this was
when "Jewish 'capital' came into conflict with all classes
of society."[88] As Fernand Braudel asserts,"The chief cul-
prit was the general recession of the western world. On
this point it seems to me that no argument is possible."[89]

d) In Sephardic country

It is a known fact, says Cecil Roth, that "as far back as the Roman period, the Jews of the Peninsula had been numerous and influential."[90] And Shlomo Sand suggests the possibility that "Judaism probably began to germinate in the Iberian Peninsula in the early centuries CE, mainly among proselytized Roman soldiers, slaves and merchants — much as it did in other imperial colonies in the northwestern Mediterranean."[91] "Of course ... the state religion was Christianity but Judaism", notes Béatrice Leroy, "was tolerated in the Roman Empire just as it was in the barbarian kingdoms that succeeded it."[92] "Thus early on", she adds, "Christians and Jews were on such close and familiar terms with one another that the Council of Elvira (near Granada) from 300 to 305 forbade Christians to share meals with Jews, such was the ease with which conviviality seemed to foster conversion."[93] "The Visigoths embraced the Arian form of Christianity, and tended to favour the Jews both as strict monotheists and as an influential minority"[94] observes Cecil Roth, as does Jean Descola who for his part notes that "most Jews had achieved an enviable position under the shadow of Arianism. Almost all of them had grown rich."[95] By converting to Catholicism, the Visigothic kings, "began to show the traditional zeal of the neophyte. The Jews were the first to suffer"[96] notes Cecil Roth. In 681, the Council of Toledo having undertaken to stamp out the "Jewish plague", many a Jew converted while many others fled to find refuge in North Africa. As Descola relates, "a few years before the Moslem invasion, the Spanish Jews reached an understanding with their African brothers. Together they planned an uprising against the Visigothic monarchy; the Berbers were to disembark and move in from the coast. When the plot was discovered, even sterner measures were brought to bear against the Jews."[97]

When the Muslims landed in 711, they were welcomed as liberators. "The thundering victory of Gibraltar was a victory for the Jew"[98] as Descola asserts.

"When the Muslims first conquered immense territories and were a tiny minority of conquerors amid a vast majority of the conquered, they needed security precautions for the protection of the occupying and governing elements"[99] explains Bernard Lewis. Thus from the outset, "the first great Arab conqueror, 'Umar ... gave orders that the institutions of subject lands were to be respected"[100] notes Joseph Calmette. However, on closer inspection, "what began as security restrictions became social and legal disabilities"[101] observes Lewis, who lists among other restrictions: a ban on bearing arms, building new churches and synagogues, and the obligation to wear special emblems on clothes, disclosing that "this, incidentally, is the origin of the yellow badge, which was first introduced by a caliph in Baghdad in the ninth century and spread into Western lands in later medieval times."[102] Alexandre Skirda pinpoints the caliph in question as Umar II whose pact enforcing "the adoption of a special emblem — yellow for Jews, blue for Christians — dates back to the eighth century."[103] Lewis acknowledges notwithstanding that "most of these disabilities had a social and symbolic rather than a tangible and practical character."[104] In fact, as he points out, "the only real economic penalty imposed on the *dhimmīs* was fiscal."[105]

[It should be recalled here that in the "pact of 'Umar", the term *dhimmī* — on the Byzantine and Sassanid model — denoted those Christian and Jewish non-Muslims afforded toleration and protection who were allowed to practise their religion provided they did nothing to upset the majority religion in line with the custom practically everywhere at that time. "The *dhimma* was an arrangement — whether pact or grant — conceded to the community, not the individual ... . This pattern of social organization gave great authority, sometimes even power, to the leaders of the community"[106] in return, they were liable to a poll tax, the *jizya*].

On the other hand, the situation of the *dhimmī* offered many advantages. Bernard Lewis has established that "apart from the fiscal and occasionally the testamentary burden, *dhimmīs* were not subject to any disabilities. They were not barred from any occupations, nor were they forced into any others ... This led at times to a rather high proportion of non-Muslims in such occupations as diplomacy, commerce, banking, brokerage, and espionage."[107] Even though they were the subject of numerous complaints, "the practice of employing non-Muslims was and remained almost universal — for pragmatic rather than theoretical reasons. They were useful and that was enough."[108]

Thus with the capture of Gibraltar in 711 CE began the Muslim conquest of Spain. Historians, among whom Charles E. Dufourcq quoting Évariste Levi-Provençal, are inclined to detect the involvement in this event of Jews escorting and acting as "interpreters for the conquerors in the company of whose army some travelled as merchants ... just like their co-religionists who remained in the Peninsula",[109] as noted by the former. On the role of Berber regiments in the conquest, Shlomo Sand proposes that they "may well have included many proselytes who enlarged the demographic size of the older Jewish communities",[110] making the point that "contemporary Christian sources condemned the treasonable behaviour of the Jews in various cities, who welcomed the invading forces"[111] and that when "many

Christians fled, the Jews, their rivals, were appointed acting governors of many cities."[112]

In any event, as Cecil Roth acknowledges, "with the coming of the Arabs, a Golden Age was initiated for the Jews of Spain"[113] and as a result, "its communities exceeded in numbers, in culture, and in wealth, those of any other country in the whole of the western world."[114]

In Jean-Pierre Dedieu's view, "by 1050 CE, over three hundred years had elapsed and a country lay totally transformed. Spain, or rather the southern two-thirds of it, was Muslim."[115] Jean Descola makes the point that "from the eighth to the tenth century, the political geography of Spain was shaped therefore by Moslem achievement ... a spiritual wall divided Spain in two zones: Latin-Christian and Arab-Moslem."[116]

Bartolomé Bennassar notes that within this context, "throughout the eleventh, twelfth and thirteenth centuries, there existed a mutual tolerance between the three main Spanish communities: Christian, Jewish and Moorish; and within each state, dissident minorities were well received."[117] Dedieu notes however that "the year 1000 CE marked a point of no return. Shortly thereafter Al-Andalus was broken up into *taifas*, i.e. into rival, independent principalities ... of which the Christians took advantage, ... their sovereigns had put their armies in the service of Moslem kinglets, growing considerably richer as a consequence."[118] In exchange for their protection, the *taifas* had to pay large amounts of tribute money, which led to their ruin. "Seeing no way out, and urged on by their subjects whose religious zeal grew as the danger increased, [the kings of the *taifas*] had resolved to call in the fundamentalist Almoravides* who had just seized power in Morocco, having swept aside the *taifas* ... crushed the

---

* *Almoravides: literally, deeply religious person, hermit (al-murabit).*

Christian armies"[119] adds Dedieu. In their wake, the Almohades* would sweep in, Islamized Berbers "even more focused on throwing out the infidel and saving Al-Andalus."[120] Thus for more than a century was the bastion of Christian Spain, Toledo, under siege, and Madrid under threat. On the 16th July 1195 the allied Christian army overcame the Almohad troops at Las Navas de Tolosa and "at a stroke the border was advanced two hundred kilometres to the south: Toledo had found peace at last."[121] "Now the frontier city between Christianity and Islam, Toledo was henceforth the base from which the assaults of the Reconquista would be launched. ... How can a city in a semi-permanent state of war also be a place of tolerance, religious co-existence and culture?"[122] wondered Louis Cardaillac.

The point is made by Jean-Pierre Dedieu that in fact "many Moslems had fled. The Mozarab** community, doubtless the largest in Spain, seized part of the émigrés' possessions. The large Jewish community was there to a man in its compound. The surrender was marked by liberality: everybody, including Muslims, kept their possessions and their religion",[123] adding that "very soon, however, migrants from the North, often from France"[124] came to settle in the city that the king handed over to them. From 1063, "the pope had been granting indulgences to whoever would go to Spain to fight the infidels",[125] so much so that in "1212 a large army collected in Toledo ... , an unruly mob, greedy for plunder, urged on by the preaching of clerics."[126] The remainder of the kingdom was to fall in the years to come. "In 1230, Ferdinand III permanently united the two kingdoms."[127] "That left

---

* Almohades: literally, "monotheist" (almuadid).
** Mozarab (or Arabized), name given to the Christians of Spain who, keeping their religion and their laws under Muslim rule, spoke Arabic and through whom many Arabic terms passed into Castilian Spanish.

Granada. It was captured in 1492 by the Catholic kings.
Its fall signalled the end of the political existence of Islam
in Europe but not its religious being. Indeed, the terms
granted to its inhabitants bore a strange resemblance to
those laid down to Toledo four hundred years before
… Just how the times had moved on could be quickly
gauged: from 1501, agreements were declared null and
void, followed by the forced conversion of the majority
of the population to Christianity …In 1610, the *Moriscos*[*],
descendants of the Spanish Moors … were finally driv-
en from the kingdom in appalling conditions: 160,000
people went into exile"[128] as Jean-Pierre Dedieu explains.
Bartolomé Bennassar reports that "during the 75 years
prior to their expulsion, they served as the chief prey for
the Inquisitors of Valencia, Saragossa and Granada."[129]

Yosef Hayim Yerushalmi notes that "certainly it
was only because they were indispensable to the economy that the New Christians of the seventeenth century
did not share the fate of the *Moriscos*, expelled by Philip
III in 1609."[130]

e) Reconquest and "New Christians"

In Yosef Hayim Yerushalmi's view, "the Marranos
have, after all, both a "Peninsular" and a "Jewish" history, and it is not surprising that the two aspects have often
been treated as separate entities",[131] pointing out that the
Marranos "had, in a sense, two lives, one prior to their
departure, and another subsequent to it."[132]

Esther Benbassa and Aron Rodrigue stress that

---

[*] *False converts for the most part.*

"most of the history of the Jews in Christian Spain can be seen within the perspective of the unfolding of this "royal alliance". The high points corresponded to the period of greatest need for the Jews by centralized authority. The nadir was reached with deteriorating circumstances associated with momentary losses of royal power or with the abandonment of the Jews by the center upon finding itself obliged to yield to pressures coming from other forces in society"[133] and conclude that "precisely the same circumstances that had made the Jews indispensable for many Muslim kingdoms also became significant in the new *Reconquista* kingdoms."[134]

Thus, according to Riccardo Calimani, did Hasdai ibn Shaprut (915-970) become "the first Jewish courtier in Cordoba, in Muslim Spain",[135] whose example was followed "in the next century by Samuel ha-Nagid who became one of the foremost dignitaries at the court of Granada."[136] Alfonso VI, King of Castile and Leon, who had taken back Toledo in 1085, "valued the role of the Jews and drew up a set of laws and local customs called *fueros* that re-established civil equality by allowing Jews access to the full range of political and public offices."[137] For their part, the pious Almoravides, "rivalling the kings of Castile, Aragon and Navarre in this respect",[138] were politically liberal, "bestowing the title of vizir or *naghid* [prince] on many Jews."[139] Pilar León Tello points out that "in Toledo, Jews still held public offices of Arab origin, like that of *alguazil* which took a number of forms: the *alguazil sahibaxorta* led a body of city police; the *alguazil alhakim* was a judge acting on the alcalde's authority. The *almojarife* was a far more important figure. His remit was vague, but included the levying of taxes ... stewardship of the royal estate, overseeing army supplies."[140] When all was said and done, "*the Reconquista* was, hence, accompanied by the confirmation of the privileges of the Jews and in fact by their extension."[141]

As a rule, in Bartolomé Bennassar's overview, "Jews, by virtue of their numbers and social position, achieved a privileged status within medieval Castilian society. They formed what was essentially an urban bourgeoisie, monopolizing commercial and financial affairs",[142] further pointing to the obvious fact that "most Jews led nondescript and humble lives behind their business shutters."[143] For, while "some of them took advantage of these high appointments in order to favour their co-religionists, others exploited their influence for their own personal gain ... their attitude", notes Pilar León Tello, "aroused a certain resentment among the Jewish popular classes, and even more so among the Christians who, from the thirteenth century onwards, fought against the favour in which sovereigns and magnates held such people."[144]

Among its Muslims and within Jewish and Christian camps alike, Spain was in other respects affected by heresy. Riccardo Calimani notices that in a thirteenth century marked by intolerance, "Christian society entertained ambiguous attitudes towards the Jews."[145] He affirms that "the Church did not yet seek their destruction but their more or less forced conversion."[146] Pilar León Tello counters that "nothing suggests that the archbishops intended to evangelize Moors and Jews, and a model of tolerance was instanced in the way Toledans defended their Jewish fellow citizens when they were attacked in 1212 by French Crusaders who had come to take part in the Navas de Tolosa campaign."[147] Similarly, Henry Charles Lea mentions that "although Jews as a class were not liable to persecution by the Inquisition, still, if after being once converted they reverted to Judaism, or if they proselyted among Christians to obtain converts from

Christianity, they were heretics in the eyes of the Church, they fell under inquisitorial jurisdiction and were liable to be abandoned to the secular arm",[148] indeed just like "the Christian who turns Jew or Moslem is legally a heretic, and is to be burned, as well as one who brings up a child in the forbidden faith."[149] He stresses however that "Castile continued unvexed by the Inquisition, and persecution for heresy was almost unknown ... . The great kingdom of Castile and Leon, embracing the major portion of the Spanish peninsula, never enjoyed the blessing of the mediaeval Inquisition."[150]

As Benbassa and Rodrigue observe, "the economic crisis of the 1380s and sharpening class conflict added fuel to the growing hostility of the population toward the Jews",[151] with Henry Charles Lea noting that "the main trouble lay in the multitudes of Jews and Moors who, under the law, were entitled to toleration, but whom popular fanaticism had forced to conversion in great numbers",[152] as indeed happened in Seville in 1391. "Outbreaks were avoided only in Moslem Granada and, thanks to the vigorous measures of protection taken by the Crown in Portugal."[153]

Thereafter, as Bartolomé Bennassar points out, "all cities with *aljamas* (Jewish and Muslim-only compounds) were swept along by this movement ... . From the outset, the increasing numbers of those converted by force rather than religious conviction were regarded as false Christians who continued to practise their former religion in secret. New words appeared in street vocabulary to denote them: *Marrano, Judaizer and converso*."[154]

According to Riccardo Calimani, from the fourteenth century onwards "the Church, in league with converted Jews led a wholesale offensive against Judaism: eradication, not persuasion, was now the order of the day"[155] further observing on this score that "Judaism was

divided: Jews regarded the "New Christians", whether
zealous converts to their new faith or secret Judaizers,
as traitors and renegades";[156] citing the example of the ri-
ots in 1395, when "the Archbishop of Toledo sought to
appoint his physician Don Pedro as chief judge over the
Jews in his archdiocese"[157] the very fact that Don Pedro
was a convert unleashed a storm of protest. The general furore and uproar in the synagogue gave way to a
pitched battle."[158]

"The social status enjoyed by the new class of *conversos* was nevertheless on a par with that of the Jews"
maintains Bennassar: "this class monopolized not only
commercial and financial activity but also a substantial
number of top administrative posts in the municipal
councils, the medical profession and a large number of
handicrafts."[159] Moreover, "baptism opened other, previously closed doors to it such as ecclesiastical and court
appointments."[160] Cecil Roth notes that "it was now out of
the question to exclude them from any walk of life on the
ground of their creed. The Law, the administration, the
army, the universities, the Church itself, were all overrun
by recent converts of more or less questionable sincerity,
or by their immediate descendants",[161] instancing "Pablo
de Santa Maria, who, as Solomon ha-Levi, had at one time
been a rabbi, but subsequently rose to the dignity of Bishop of his native Burgos, and member of the Council of
Regency of Castile",[162] or "Bonafus [ibn Labi de la Cabal-
leria] … the author of a fiercely anti-Jewish work, *Zelus
Christi contra Judaeos et Sarracenos* (Zeal of Christ against
the Jews, and Saracens) … In 1464, he was assassinated
— possibly at the instigation of his fellow-Marranos."[163]

"From then on, crypto-Judaism was destined
to be seen as a threat and a trigger for acute pathologi-
cal reactions that were to turn a Spain obsessed by the
restoration of blood purity [*limpieza*] upside down",[164]

explains Riccardo Calimani. For, as Bartolomé Bennassar elucidates, "the conversions had an increasingly
meaningful purpose: that of favouring mixed marriages
between Old and New Christians that furnished an entrée
into the Castilian and Aragonese nobility."[165] In this way,
"the *conversos* founded powerful dynasties and aroused
a sense of unease among the nobility keen to hold on to
their privileges."[166]

Bennassar goes on to relate that in 1449 "a petition
submitted to the Bishop of Cuenca declared that Jewish
blood flowed through the veins of the noblest families of
Spain … especially those of the Henriquez from whom
Ferdinand the Catholic was descended on his mother's
side";[167] and that, as Jaime Contreras fittingly remarks, "the
money from a plethora of transactions was earmarked for
securing the most sought-after commodity of all: nobility.
Who would not have jumped at the chance to become a
hidalgo?"[168]

With the (January) capture of Granada, the year
1492 would mark the end of the *Reconquista*. Moreover,
"on the 31st March 1492, the Catholic monarchs signed
the edict of expulsion in the same city of Granada …
the edict gave the Jews the choice of either converting
to Christianity or else leaving Spain … Many opted for
conversion."[169] Isidoro La Lumia relates that "the fateful
edict that served a blanket expulsion order on the Jews
… began by setting out two main charges against them:
the bribing of many Christians for the purposes of luring
them into their religion and rampant moneylending"[170]
with Benbassa and Rodrigue affirming that "by 31 July
1492, the last openly practising Jew had left Spain."[171]

By Jean Descola's reckoning, "it was to Ferdinand's
credit, and his principal claim to fame, that, as soon as he
had rid the kingdom of both internal and external ene-
mies, he grew fond of his subjects and allowed Moslems

and Jews to preserve their customs, laws, and religion",[172] concluding that "both the Jews and the Arabs contributed to Spain's fund of knowledge."[173]

f) The Marrano phenomenon and its spread

Assuming, as Jean Descola states, that "among the Spanish population, composed in large part of descendants of Romans and Visigoths, many had readily become converted to Islam",[174] it should be borne in mind that it was often the very same people who had previously become converted *en masse* to Christianity. As was the case in Spain, this to-ing and fro-ing from one religion to another seems characteristic of populations who have been the target of successive invasions and have to some extent either chosen to espouse their new rulers' religion (such as the *Moriscos* or those Muslims who remained in the Peninsula after the conquest of Granada in 1492, and who converted to Christianity) or, while staying put, adopted the prevailing culture but kept their own faith (such as the *Mozarabs* or "Arabized" Christians who spoke and wrote in Arabic, or the *Mudejars*, literally "tributaries or subjects", "defeated" Muslims who remained under Christian rule), or indeed those whose determination not to submit left them no option but to leave.

On this score, Bartolomé Bennassar makes the very pertinent observation that "Islam allows those of its believers sent out into a hostile world and forced to espouse another religion to conceal their faith and disclose nothing that could compromise their lives. Thus the *takīya*, or non-expression of belief, was the means of defence against the Holy Office. A *mufti* [jurisconsult in Koranic law] from Oran's 1504 written response to the *Moriscos* of Granada ... asserted the need to dissemble in order to survive."[175] In the same way, as Cecil Roth explains, "the official attitude, as crystallized in the dicta of the Rabbis, was plain. A man might, and should, save his life if the occasion demanded it, by any means ... the concealment of Judaism, unaccompanied by any formality, was another matter."[176] Bernard Lewis draws attention to the fact that "significantly, the phenomenon of Marranism in Jewish history is virtually limited to countries of Islamic civilization or influence. The outstanding examples are the Jews of Spain and Portugal after the expulsion. Other instances are attested in Islamic lands from North Africa to Iran and Central Asia."[177]

[On this subject, the etymology of the term *Marrano* (formerly *marrone*, wild pig) "which basically means 'pork'",[178] to denote the Judaist convert is incongruous to say the least, being applied to the very people who refuse to eat it. Among those so termed, namely Jews as well as Arab converts who concealed their religious practices, *Marranos*, as can be seen from the foregoing remarks, denoted "what is not forbidden" (*ma'haram*, in Arabic). "The general population, on the other hand, used a variety of terms to describe them. They were called *conversos* ... more strictly they were denominated New Christians (*Christianos Nuevos*)."[179] (Significantly, Colombian Spanish has kept the verb *marranear* in the sense of *engañar*, i.e. to deceive, fool, dupe.[180]) The process of homonymic substitution characteristic of popular speech is thus responsible for the change of meaning here. In order to prevent backsliding, Cecil Roth recounts that even the Visigothic kings in their time had prohibited "the association of neophytes with their former co-religionists ... binding themselves to observe no Jewish rite in future; though they made an exception with respect to eating the flesh of the pig, which, they said, it was physically impossible for them to touch",[181] observing that "in spite of all these provisions, the notorious infidelity of the recent converts and their descendants remained one of the great problems of Visigothic statesmanship down to the period of the Arab invasion in 711."[182] For Roth, "the tradition of Marranism in the Peninsula had already emerged."[183]

While "most of the Jews who left in 1492 ... went to North Africa, Italy ... and into the Ottoman Empire. Many merely crossed a border, into Portugal or into Navarre",[184] recounts Béatrice Leroy who nevertheless adds that "during the winter of 1492-1493, the [Catholic] Kings made it known that they would gladly welcome back those still close to home who wished to return to familiar surroundings courtesy of baptism. New *conversos* had thus landed back in Toledo or Saragossa",[185] although she sheds no further light on such an about-turn by both sides. Cecil Roth points out elsewhere that "settled here [in Portugal] ever since the birth of the monarchy (in the thirteenth century),* Jews generally had been well-treated",[186] and that "neither the native Jews on the one hand nor the counsellors of state on the other were anxious to receive this influx."[187] However, "the ruling monarch, João II, was more friendly; though he was plainly actuated by anticipation of profit rather than by a sense of humanity."[188] In 1497 the new king Manuel I, an ally of the Catholic Kings, decreed the mass baptism of Portuguese Jews and all the exiles from Spain. From then on, writes Yosef Hayim Yerushalmi, "in Portugal, unlike Spain, there was no period of tension between *Conversos* and professing Jews, for after 1497 all who had been Jews were suddenly converts."[189] The upshot was, as Anne-Lise Polo concludes, that "forced conversion lifted all

---

* In fact, "ever since Roman times" (cf. Benbassa & Rodrigue, op. cit.)

legal impediment to the social and economic rise of the Jews in Portugal."[190]

Riccardo Calimani notes that "over the course of forty years from 1497 to 1537 when the King of Portugal, in accord with the papacy, was importing the Inquisition, Marranism had the time to develop within the kingdom."[191] Cecil Roth points out that "in 1524, a New Christian informer named Henrique Nuñes, who was acting as *agent provocateur* with the object of obtaining the introduction of the Inquisition ... had provided the king (João III) with lists of persons guilty of the practice of Judaism."[192] Yosef Hayim Yerushalmi observes that "it is in the period from 1497 to 1536 that the New Christians penetrated into the highest echelons of Portuguese commerce and finance. But it is also during this time that various modes of crypto-Jewish life became firmly entrenched among thousands of them."[193]

When in 1580, Philip II annexed Portugal to Spain, "the incursion into Spain of Portuguese New Christians was of such dimensions and impact that, to the Spaniards of the seventeenth century, "Portuguese" was virtually synonymous with "Jew"."[194] According to Yerushalmi's analysis, "in both countries the New Christians were particularly suited to fill the vacuum between a peasantry which could not rise and an aristocracy whose disdain for all forms of commercial activity was proverbial",[195] going on to point out that "we hear of some who, through their commercial contacts, managed periodically to transfer funds to Italy or Holland in preparation for their eventual departure."[196] Riccardo Calimani points out that this was how "in the sixteenth century the Marranos invaded Europe, from Amsterdam to Salonica, from Hamburg to Venice, from Florence to Rome, from Ferrara to Ancona. They spread out everywhere, even in those places where Judaism was officially banned. Others lived side by side with the Jews, sometimes blending in with them"[197] deeming that "the elusiveness of Marrano experience lies precisely therein: group destiny was replaced by count-less family and individual destinies which took shape over the course of each lifetime ... Marrano is more about men's lives and passions than about saints or martyrs."[198] For his part, Cecil Roth concluded that "the members of the Marrano Diaspora may be termed, without exaggera-tion, the first modern Jews."[199]

Venice, A City State

"Thus feudalism, a type of social organization marked by a special quality in human relationships, expressed itself not only in the creation of new institutions; it imparted its own colouring to what it received from the past, as if passing it through a prism, and transmitting it to succeeding ages."
Marc Bloch, *Feudal Society*

"Venice, the city of merchants, escaped mercantilism by the grace of an affliction that its ancestor Byzantium had passed on to it … : a passion for endurance."
Frédérick Tristan, *Venice*

a) Expansion

According to the legend that subsequently took shape, Venice was founded on the 25th March (Lady Day), 421 on the islets of the *rivus altus* [deep stream] by Romanized populations from the Terra ferma fleeing the

Huns. As for the founding myth, Jean-Claude Hocquet makes the point that it is "linked to the arrival of Saint Mark in Aquileia, an event that was chronicled only much later on (end of the eighth century) … from then on, Venice became Saint Mark's city, as Rome is Saint Peter's."[1]

Staying with the historical record, Freddy Thiriet points out that "when the generals under Justinian (emperor of the East from 527 to 565) had reconquered Italy in 555, the province of Venetia and Istria quite naturally rejoined the Roman union."[2] Only in 568, with the Lombard invasion, did "everything change … . In a few years, Byzantine rule in Padanian Italy was over … , whereupon there began the massive exodus that the chronicles speak of, during which time the inhabitants of Padua, Aquileia and Altino took refuge under cover of the lagoons in Malamocco, around the Realtine islands, the seat of the future Venice or further to the east at Grado."[3]

It remained the case that "Venice was unquestionably considered part of the Byzantine Empire even after the Lombards had captured Ravenna in 751."[4] And in the following century, the peace treaty concluded between Charlemagne and the Greek Emperor (in 812) explicitly acknowledged that the Duchy of Venice (the *dogado*) — which had just established its seat at Rialto in the Doges' Palace — reverted to the Byzantine Empire.

Subsequently, given that "the suzerainty of the Byzantine emperor gradually faded away",[5] nevertheless, "the Venetians refused pointedly to acknowledge subordination to any of the Germanic tribal kings who in the West used the title of Holy Roman Emperor to sanctify and extend their power."[6]

Egle Trincinato indicates that "in the eleventh century, the chronicle of Giovanni Diacono gave the name of "city" to the built-up area that stretched over the left bank of the Grand Canal to the east of San Marco as far as Rivoalto."[7]

According to Philippe Braunstein and Robert Delort's description of the city, "Venice, which was in contact with several areas of production and consumption, took advantage of its position as an intermediary between the western world, on whose fringes it was moored; the Byzantine world, to which the very conditions of its emergence attached it; the Slav world that it could access directly via Istria and Dalmatia, thereafter via the Black Sea as well as indirectly via Germania; the Islamic world via Sicily until the Norman conquest, thereafter via Barbary, Syria and Egypt; and finally the lands of Mongolia and the Far East in the thirteenth and fourteenth centuries whether by direct routes or via Islamic territory."[8] Frederic C. Lane is thus prompted to remark that "being on the edge of two worlds — the Byzantine and Moslem East and the Latin-Germanic West — Venetians looked sometimes eastward, at other times westward for profits and power and for artistic inspiration."[9] Nevertheless, as Christian Bec observes, it was "with Constantinople that the Doge established close and secure ties by placing his sea power at the service of the empire of the East."[10] So much so that, as Élisabeth Crouzet-Pavan outlines, "the 993 agreement had already stipulated that Venice would receive customs privileges in return for future military aid, but in 1082 Emperor Alexius I Comnenus made even greater concessions",[11] adding that, "first, in its tenure, the present chrysobull listed several "liberalities", concessions that, although far from negligible, were nonetheless in the domain of honour. Next came economic concessions, which were considerable."[12] "The Venetian colony in Constantinople ... was granted sizable improvements in its infrastructure: ... storage facilities and three anchorage sites on the Golden Horn ... . In numerous places and ports throughout the imperial territories the Venetians were granted the right to trade freely, with no impediment and no customs duties."[13]

Thus did "Venetian emigration reach Mediterranean trading ports at the end of the eleventh century at the very latest."[14] Its temporary aspect was due to the "developmental and transformative" effect of the *Crusades* on it."[15] Following the conquest of Constantinople in 1204, this settlement became permanent, and the residential and storage concessions, indeed the use of whole districts, formed the veritable enclaves of extraterritoriality referred to above.

Jean-Claude Hocquet draws attention to another distinctive feature in that "while the concept of "nation" enjoyed limited currency during the Middle Ages, Venice used naturalization for the benefit of foreigners",[16] specifying that "the granting of Venetian "nationality", however, fulfilled political objectives: to bring about an increase in the number of Venetians in order to be stronger and more feared, although its intended recipients were above all those who acted as middlemen between merchants and the local population."[17] Hocquet nevertheless underlines that "naturalization in no way implied "integration", Venetian citizens clinging jealously to their social supremacy; naturalization was only of value in the dependencies but marriage with a Venetian woman, services rendered, and a few years spent in the home city could entitle one to citizenship."[18]

In Pierre Moukarzel's analysis, by virtue of their minority status, the trading nations represented "a bone of contention between the authorities and the people",[19] adding that "they certainly achieved an acknowledged status, but the latter was fragile and unstable ... necessary only to the ruling class whose interest lay in the smooth running of the trade that filled State coffers",[20] although "on the other hand, as far as the majority of the population was concerned, merchants were regarded as intruders in Muslim lands because of their different religion and culture."[21] "Being Christian, foreign and wealthy, they were subjected to sordid physical abuse and mass reprisals"[22] reminiscent here and there of those meted out to the Jews.

b) La Dominante

In her book on Venice, Donatella Calabi refers to "a commercial civilization whose increase in power was measured against the creation of trade routes, the settlement of citizens further and further away from their home city, and the mixing together of populations each with their own language, culture and traditions."[23] According to the Venetian printer-publisher Franco Filippi, "the real magic of Venice was its ability to get people of every kind and every creed to live together in mutual restraint within a limited area."[24]

On an institutional level, Marie F. Viallon explains that "in the early stages of its history, Venice was a city where the people — in the sense of a large representation of the population — had the power to ratify decrees and laws through the exercise of its *placitum* (plea or approval) and the mission to elect the Doge. It would not be long, however, before such power passed into select hands among the great patrician families."[25]

"City life was organized around a large number of parishes [*Contrade*]"[26] notes Donatella Calabi. Frederic C. Lane stresses that "the integration within these parishes was a foundation stone of Venice's social stability. The preservation of neighbourhood spirit after Venice grew more populous is one more reason for considering Venice a model of city planning."[27] Lewis Mumford marvels that "each neighbourhood or parish reproduces on a smaller scale the essential organs of the bigger, all-embracing city, with the maximum possibilities for meeting and association on every human level, all within walking distance of the centre"[28] and compares Venice to the capital of Thomas More's "*Utopia*". As Lane affirms, "notoriously, modern cities are more successful as places in which to make a living than as places to live. Venice was successful in both ways."[29]

In Marie F. Viallon's analysis, "no longer was Venice some little town tucked away in an imperial no-man's-land and peopled by fugitives of varying degrees of nobility permanently under Byzantine rule. Ever since the *Maggior Consiglio* decree of the 9th May 1462, it changed the title of its *Comune en Dominium* state, i.e. it now put its political independence, institutional freedom, and its control over mainland possessions such as the Stato del Mar running from Istria to the shores of the Black Sea, on world display."[30] Viallon compares this expansion to "a net spread over the Mediterranean whose knots represented trading posts, warehouses and stores, and whose ropes were the sea routes linking them all up, together with the focal point for every merchandise in the commercial quarter of Rialto."[31]

c) A State in the service of merchants

Lewis Mumford makes the point that "the very word merchant does not appear in Mesopotamian writings till the second millennium",[32] when it "'designates the official of a temple privileged to trade abroad'".[33]

As Philippe Braunstein and Robert Delort define it, "Venice was not only a city of trade but also a State of traders, a State in the service of traders. Safe from political vagaries, an admirable organization defended the interest of the collectivity, while safeguarding individual endeavour."[34] Bernard Doumerc affirms nevertheless that "in reality, Venice developed a set of highly monopolistic and interventionist policies",[35] and "the city's omnipresent wealth mainly benefited the wealthiest Venetians",[36] in other words the nobles who ruled the city and who "formed a merchant caste, jealous of its power."[37]

But what in fact is the case here? Jean-Claude Hocquet points out that "in Venice, a city founded not on soil, but on the sea which belongs to nobody *(res nullius)*, neither pope nor emperor nor anybody else for that matter could lay claim to the *dominium* — a word that could be translated as "sovereignty" — such *dominium* belonging as a right to whoever appropriates it."[38] *Citizens* are therefore the ones who "enjoy this right of property which forms the basis of their freedom and their leave to trade in Venice, the duchy and throughout the dominions, in Dalmatia and Romania."[39] Around 1520 in *The Commonwealth and Government of Venice,* Gasparo Contarini declared that "the bulk of the people are divided into two categories, of which the most honourable is that of citizen, the other being formed of the lower orders, that is to say craftsmen and the like", feeling certain, as Frederic C. Lane stipulates, that "only those we call nobles [were citizens]",[40] basing "citizenship (nobility) strictly on ancestry, not on wealth."[41]

In fact a middle class tends increasingly to differentiate itself from the popular classes and, similarly, "within this middle class, the highest status, although not necessarily the largest fortunes, belonged to those called "native-born citizens" [*cittadini originari or de jure*],"[42] "others of the native-born citizens engaged in international trade with the same rights as the nobility"[43] explains F. C. Lane. In a higher category were the cives, "immigrants for the most part … who had been granted citizenship as a privilege",[44] although as Jean-Claude Hocquet makes clear, "in order to derive any benefit from it, two conditions had to be met: a permanent abode and enough income to qualify as a taxpayer … being a Christian was also mandatory since being a Jew meant automatic ineligibility, although nowhere was there any explicit formulation of this rule."[45]

Hocquet further points out that supposing "the privileged outcome of naturalization to be the very widespread right to open and run shops by trading within and outside Venice, commercial relations with "foreigners" were nevertheless kept under tight regulation."[46] However, Reinhold Mueller draws attention to the fact that on the basis of archival research, "however unusual it may appear, those immigrants declaring Germanic lands as their country of origin numbered no more than fifty or so, underlining the fact that the two-way commercial privileges based on the structure of the renowned Fondaco dei Tedeschi afforded merchants more advantages than naturalization did."[47]

d) Fondaci

Different types of *fondaci* have existed ever since their creation in the Middle Ages for the ongoing purposes of levying dues and stockpiling essential supplies. Hence the *Fondaco del Miglio* [millet], and those stocking

salt, flour, oil, wine, etc. As Jean-Claude Hocquet observes, "Stores of essential supplies were strategically
located throughout the city in readiness for any eventuality",[48] stressing that "granaries and *fontichi*, protected
by canals, were encircled by crenelles and merlons",[49]
like the salt shops on the Punta della Dogana: "the latter,
whose extensive façades overlooked the Grand and the
Giudecca Canals, were defended by one of the few towers to be found in Venice."[50]

Élisabeth Crouzet-Pavan mentions that at the end
of the eleventh century, the Orio family, "aristocratic
owners of the first commercial installations on the Rialto island, solemnly deeded [*"For the honour of the market
and the length and breadth of our country"*] the family lands
and the buildings on them to the city. The act drawn
up to sanction this gift called this space a "market",[51] to
which Donatella Calabi adds "thus there emerged an area
protected and controlled by the commune, i.e. by those
magistracies responsible respectively for law and order,
the collection of dues and taxes, the supervision of the
Arts and Crafts and maintenance corporations. This area,
which was devoted to the trade in foodstuffs and general
domestic wares, also became the privileged location for
sealing international trade agreements."[52]

"As far as possible, some of the goods freight passing through Venice to its mainland possessions was con-
veyed by sea."[53]

Moreover, as Braunstein and Delort point out, "on
the one hand, Venice was in regular contact, via the Rhine
valley, with Bruges and, in the fifteenth century, with
Antwerp; on the other, with Vienna, Breslau and Cracow.
Northwards of the Alps, Venetian merchandise circulat-
ed much more frequently than Venetians themselves did.
Instead, merchants from Germanic lands came to Venice
to obtain supplies."[54] Alvise Zorzi draws attention to the

"densely built-up and heavily populated area of Rialto from the thirteenth to the sixteenth centuries [which] was the most extraordinary melting pot of languages, people, races, and also the most active and colourful centre of large and small-scale business ever seen since the decline of Constantinople",[55] going on to instance "the colonies of non-Venetian merchants ... , mainland Venetians, together with those from Istria, Dalmatia, Romagna, Emilia, the Marches, Abruzzi, and Apulia, not to mention the Florentines ..., the Luccans ..., many Greeks, Albanians, Slavs, and even French. However, by far the most numerous without any shadow of a doubt were the Germans, established in their warehouse which, even after the relocation of the market, had remained on the other side of the canal in San Bartolomio."[56]

Donatella Calabi indicates that from the twelfth century onward, "the private dwellings of great merchants would serve increasingly as commercial premises and goods depots ... . Ever since the early *fondaci*-dwellings of the Middle Ages, building had comprised ever higher and more complex structures ... . An amalgam of *fondaco* and private dwelling ... Venice still possesses some magnificent examples of these merchants' houses: the Ca' (lineal dwelling place) Foscolo at Pantalon, the Ca' Falier at Santi Apostoli, the Ca' da Mosto, Donà, Pesaro, Farsetti, Loredan on the Grand Canal ... . They were often lavishly decorated."[57]

According to the historical atlas *"Venise au fil du temps"* [Venice Down Through the Ages], *"fondaci* and residential buildings (from about 1250 onwards) were erected to house migrants from Venetia, Lombardy, Emilia, the Marches, Tuscany and Europe (especially Germans and Jews)."[58]

Between 1222 and 1225, the Signoria awarded a building to the "German nation": the *Fondaco dei Te-*

deschi (or *fontico dalamia)*, situated at the foot of the Rialto bridge. Both warehouse and compulsory place of residence, the building was inspired by the *fonduks* of Muslim countries, "also called caravanserais or *khan*, a term of Persian origin"[59] as Anne Raulin explains, and reserved for foreign merchants. Bernard Doumerc describes their workings thus: "once in the city, the merchant lived in a State-owned warehouse-inn ... . He laid down his arms and went to see the resident Venetian customs house functionaries and the commissioners for contracts. He would get in touch with Venetian courtiers and interpreters, then enter into transactions ... : present his available funds and his merchandise for inspection since he was forbidden to import English or Flemish goods under regulations protecting the *muda** traffic of Flanders. Lastly, negotiations could be conducted only with Venetians within the *fonduk*. Before leaving the city, he would settle the bill for his accommodation, leave any unsold stock on the premises and entrust any surplus cash to representatives."[60]

Following its rebuilding in the early fourteenth century, Élisabeth Crouzet-Pavan describes [the *Fondaco dei Tedeschi*] to us as "two storeys high, with three inner courtyards. ... [it was] almost as big as the current building which was erected in the sixteenth century"[61] (in the wake of a fire one winter's night in 1505). However, in René Guerdan's judgement, "as fine as it was, the fondaco was a prison ... at night, they were locked in from the outside."[62]

"More unassuming from an architectural point of view and also overlooking the Grand Canal, the *Fondaco dei Persiani* [Ca' Ruzzini , on the corner of the Grand Canal, dating from 1400 and demolished in 1908] ... had

---

* *Convoy of galleys of the State-organized line.*

adopted the same kind of configuration around a squareish and enclosed courtyard"[63] notes Donatella Calabi, adding that in the case of the *Fondaco dei Turchi*, "despite appearing to be designed along the same lines, it was in fact the reorganization of a former privately-owned palazzo."[64]

Concerning the Turks, Julian Raby stresses that "Venice was the only city in Europe that for several centuries received a regular stream of Ottoman dignitaries and visitors, and Venice was the only city, with the exception of Ancona, where there was an established presence of Turkish merchants and Ottoman subjects from domains such as the Balkans. There were a good number of Ottoman Muslim merchants in Venice at the outbreak of the war in 1571 [the Battle of Lepanto], and after the declaration of peace in 1573, their numbers rose until it was finally decided in 1612, following increasingly popular complaints, that it was disruptive for them to continue to occupy different residences, including houses of ill-repute"[65] (like that of the *calle dell'Angelo*, near the Rialto), "although Asiatic Turks protested against having to live with Balkan Turks, claiming that their customs were so different they were sure there would be fights"[66] Frederic C. Lane indicates. In 1618, the State acquired the Palazzo of the Dukes of Ferrara in order to lay out the new *Fondaco dei Turchi* within its walls. "Orders were given to lock all doors and windows except for the main gate that opened onto the public highway; to forbid entry to women and fresh-faced youths, to gunpowder and firearms, etc."[67] For its part, the *Fondaco dei Servi* housed Slavs.

"The tenement block constitutes a favoured field for the mass settlement of foreigners"[68] notes Jean-François Chauvard, "an environment seeming to offer optimum fulfilment of the foreigner's desire to be with other foreigners", thus "the variations that may be observed in the density of this built environment arise from the conjunction of available space that the owner has on offer with the foreigner's desire for close professional, family, and community proximity",[69] noting too that "population size and community renewal are no less decisive factors."[70]

Donatella Calabi stresses the fact that "the policy of the Venetian bench was characterized by a concern for control and the offer of safeguards to every foreigners' association."[71] It is the case, moreover, that "the solution evidenced in the assignment of Jews to an outlying district, where their freedom of movement could be monitored, was not that unusual. After all, the same logic underpinned the institution of the *fondaci* for foreign nations. The situation was on a par with other communities such as the Greeks or Albanians who would organize themselves into tight-knit settlements."[72]

*e) "Siamo Veneziani, poi cristiani"**

"Because of the strength of the Byzantine tradition of subordinating the clergy"[73] and, as Frederic C. Lane grants, "although, like other medieval Christians, the Venetians thought of themselves as a religious community, ... they looked to the doge rather than to any ecclesiastic as the head of that community",[74] whereas "other Italian city states of the later Middle Ages acknowledged a theoretical sovereignty of the emperor or pope."[75] Henry Charles Lea asserts, however, that "that policy held at bay in all things the pretensions of the Holy See, and looked with extreme suspicion on whatever might give the popes

---

* *"We are Venetians first, Christians second"*.

an excuse for interference with either the domestic policy or the foreign enterprises of the Signoria."[76] Lea further contends that "fairly orthodox, though not bigoted,
… the republic made no haste to join in the movement
for the extermination of heresy so energetically pushed
by Gregory IX [pope from 1227 to 1241] and his successors"[77] so that "as the pressure of the Inquisition extended
throughout Lombardy and the Marches, the persecuted
heretics naturally sought a refuge in Venetian territory."[78]
In 1288, Pope Nicholas IV commanded that the doge, on
pain of excommunication, "should swear not only not to
impede the Inquisitor of Treviso in his duties, but to assist
him."[79] This was followed by the ratification of a compromise whereby the State, by keeping all the Holy Office
expenses for itself, was at the same time in a position to
exercise its own control. Lea notes that as consequence,
"heresy … continued to flourish in Venetian territory",[80]
adding that "in Calabria, in 1530, it was estimated that
[heretics] numbered ten thousand souls, in Venetia, six
thousand."[81]

As Frederic C. Lane acknowledges, "the Venetian
tradition was distinctive"[82] in that "although bishops
served as chief ministers in most West European states,
in Venice they were excluded from all political office … .
Church property in Venice was taxed, and clerics accused
of crimes were judged in state courts."[83]

Marie F. Viallon notes that "Venetians considered
that they neither ran nor controlled Church estates and
neither should the pope run or control matters of criminal
law on Venetian territory."[84] Thus on the 6th May 1606,
"Jesuits, Capuchins and Theatines received orders to leave
Venice."[85] Under Paul V (1605-1621), the doge "systemat-
ically stood in the Inquisition's way every time it tried
to introduce legal measures against the Jews, or far more
frequently, against Judaizing Marranos",[86] as Riccardo

Calimani observes.

"Protestantism was tolerated only marginally as ... the religious custom of a few foreigners: the German merchants in their Fondaco, a flourishing colony of German bakers, and the many German students at Padua."[87]

Elsewhere, "for its Greek Orthodox colony, the government won from Rome the right for them to use their own calendar. Jews and Moslems performed their own rites in their special quarters or hostels ... . But men of a great variety of views succeeded in one way or another in living in Venice pretty much as they pleased, and thinking as they pleased, so long as they did not attack the government."[88] Franco Filippi gives us an illustration of a case in point when he relates that "after the Council of Florence in 1437, the substantial and respected Greek delegation which had travelled to Italy in order to break the deadlock surrounding the earlier East-West schism in the Church, declared its trust in the Jews and their culture. Jewish thought in the first instance with the study of literature and then of language ... had found free expression within the learned society of nobles which included clerical figures such as Cardinal Domenico Grimani and Brother Francesco Zorzi."[89]

Élisabeth Crouzet-Pavan grants that "the city had always been open"[90] and "thanks to migrations from the Terra ferma and the mountainous areas inland ... it overcame the population losses of the fourteenth century",[91] due for the most part, it will be recalled, to the epidemic of the Black Death that tore through Europe from 1347 to 1351, followed by the so-called "Venetian plague" of 1478. She notes accordingly that "wars, plagues, famines and heavenly portents, all the chronicles subsequent to Charles VIII's first incursion into Italy in 1495 give the same doom-mongering account of Italian misfortunes",[92] making the point that "in a thorough-going defence of overwhelmingly Christian interests, the Council of Ten ordered its guards for example to protect the houses of Jews in Mestre containing pawned goods."[93] Frederic C. Lane has explained that "after seven years of war, in which many of its cities had been sacked and the countryside ravaged, Venice regained in 1516 the essentials of the territory it had won on the mainland almost a century earlier ... . By her diplomacy as much as by her arms she defended herself against the Renaissance monarchs who plundered and subjected the rest of Italy."[94]

Élisabeth Crouzet-Pavan acknowledges that "in the worst moments of crisis, talks between the councils and the chief representative of the Jewish community, Anselmo, continued. This dialogue carried on in the weeks prior to the Jews' settlement in the ghetto."[95]

f) The money trade

Aron J. Gurevich writes that "in 1179 the Church officially prohibited usury to Christians. The role of the Jews in the economic life of the West can be explained above all by prohibitions of this sort"[96] making the point that "many Christians were moneylenders as well."[97] Leon Poliakov confirms that "during the thirteenth century, in fact, and a good part of the fourteenth, short-term lending and pawnbroking were practised in Italy by both Christians and Jews. Later, however, Jews supplanted 'Lombards', or 'Tuscans' and ended up by ousting them completely ... . Outside Italy ... the evolution, particularly in Western Europe, might even be said to be the reverse ... . In the Netherlands, the Lombard dynasties ended up by monopolizing consumption loans."[98] According to Benjamin Nelson, "the merchant-usurer of the early Middle Ages had been broken down to yield two disparate figures who stood at opposite poles: the ... manifest usurer-pawnbroker, as often as not a Jew; and the city father ... a merchant prince."[99]

The fifteenth General Council that opened in 1311 in Vienne to debate heresy and the fate of the Templars declared that all those who sought to justify usury were heretics, whereupon "usury inspired the preachers to an incommensurable wrath",[100] and, as Aron J. Gurevich also points out, "the persecution and slaughter of Italian usurers, in particular in France during the late thirteenth and fourteenth centuries, were phenomena as frequent and widespread as pogroms against the Jews."[101] Leon Poliakov for his part emphasizes "the contrast ... between the Christian usurer living in a state of permanent sin, condemned by the Church, and the Jewish usurer whose activities were entirely justified in the eyes of the rabbis",[102] going on to explain that "from the moment when 'overt and public usury' aroused general disapproval, the ardour put into making money this way was of necessity somewhat chilled by the disrepute which was attached to it — to the greater advantage of the Jewish lenders",[103] and concluding that "in short, it seems that the Christian 'public usurers' did not finally disappear from the scene until the end of the fifteenth century, when the first Monti di Pietà appeared and multiplied in Italian cities ... . Christian lenders were able to forbid Jews access to these towns for many generations."[104] However, "in Venice the situation was different since the city was off-limits to Christian and Jewish pawnbrokers alike."[105]

g) The stakes of the "condotta"

"At Venice — which in this, as in so many other points, sets the example — ", Leon Poliakov notes, "the monopoly of pawnbroking was granted to Jews (Germans in all probability) in 1366. Such were the origins of the 'Banchi dei Poveri', the famous Venetian pawnshops. In the Most Serene Republic, this form of social assistance remained the province of the Jews until the beginning of the nineteenth century",[106] mentioning also that "the first agreements concluded by the small towns or *castelli* in central Italy with the Jews of Rome seem to date from the second half of the thirteenth century. By the terms of these agreements, called *condotte*, the Jews could settle in the city, lend at interest and on security there (at a statutory rate which varied according to the place, the amount of the loan, etc.), engage in all types of business and have complete freedom to practise their religion … . In return, they were obliged to invest a certain sum of capital in the *banco*, to pay an annual fee proportional to this capital to the commune, and, when necessary, to advance funds to it at a reduced rate."[107] These temporary *condotte* were the preserve of the *banchieri*. Cecil Roth makes it clear that "other categories amongst their compatriots were treated with greater liberality, and were subject to no similar restrictions. The Levantine merchants in particular had continued to come to trade in the city as before."[108]

Jean-Claude Hocquet notes on this score that "the twenty years between 1350 and 1370 saw the Christian lending banks in Venetia disappear, ruined by the vast social network of new Jewish moneylenders who could supply a larger quantity of money more cheaply."[109] On the matter of authorized lenders, Riccardo Calimani points out that "according to the notaries' deeds, nearly all the moneylenders were Jewish ... allowed to stay [in the city] for a maximum of five years."[110] Roberta Curiel draws attention to the fact that "Jewish moneylenders congregated particularly in Treviso and Mestre, but in 1382, after lengthy negotiations, they were given the right to move to Venice with their coreligionists."[111]Although, as Calimani observes, "the new law made no distinction between Jews and Christians",[112] nevertheless "it was the beginning of the first Jewish charter."[113] On the expiry of this five-year charter, a renewal was sought. A new agreement was then reached for a period of ten years, in return for which "4,000 ducats [had] to be paid by the Jewish community, whose leaders would be independently elected and who would in turn set the quotas to be paid by individuals within the community."[114] He notes too that "the Jews were subject to no other taxes, except for the usual import-export duties ... . They were also promised an area of the town in which to live — and this, too, was a great privilege."[115] At that time, "the Jews, having thus settled in Venice, and maybe deluding themselves that the Sentence of expulsion served only for the sake of political appearances, and that they could already consider their domicile perpetual, decided to purchase a piece of land that they could use to bury their dead."[116] Despite the opposition of the Benedictine monks of the Lido, the Jews were granted a piece of land in 1389 in the neighbourhood of the San Nicolò monastery in return for an annual fee and the guarantee "that it could only be used as a cemetery"."[117]

When the charter expired in 1397, the Jews were obliged to withdraw to Mestre but as Riccardo Calimani observes, "continued coming to Venice to sell their unclaimed pledges at the Rialto",[118] adding that "they spent increasingly less time in Mestre and more in Venice, thus thwarting "the pious spirit of the Decree"."[119]As a consequence, "on the 7th September 1402, noting that the Jews were still coming and going and that they tended to congregate in certain areas of the city (Sant' Apollinare and San Silvestro), the authorities decreed that once a Jew had been in Venice for fifteen days, he could not return again for four months."[120] At the beginning of the sixteenth century, "according to Sanudo's estimate, there were about five hundred Jews in Venice ... most of them apparently living in the parishes of San Cassiano, Sant' Agostino, and San Geremia."[121] "In 1423, a new decree was enacted obliging them, within two years, to sell any real estate purchased in violation of the law",[122] prohibiting "Jews from acquiring or possessing real estate in the Venetian domains with the sole exception of la Giudecca ... . The Jews were thus obliged to keep all their assets in cash. This favoured their moneylending activities and gave them a great deal of mobility ... . At the same time, however, it also made it difficult for them to establish permanent settlements."[123] Despite this, as Calimani notes, "there is plentiful evidence that normal business negotiations, and even closer relations, were developing between individual Jews and Christians."[124] Giovanni Curatola remarks that although "there was a continuous Jewish presence in Venice despite tensions and disputes either resolved amicably or through some form of reconciliation, there is no doubt that an expulsion of wealthy Marranos accused of speculating on the Venetian staple of Sicilian wheat took place in 1497. Only a tiny minority of people, however, were involved."[125] Curatola adds that "despite the loss of many documents on the role of Jews in Venetian trade, certain surviving evidence nevertheless indicates its importance."[126]

Riccardo Calimani argues that "by the mid-fifteenth century the conditions of the Jews had improved ... The charters had given them ... relative financial comfort compared to the vast majority of the population",[127] especially since "the [general financial] situation deteriorated"[128] at this time. Alvise Zorzi underlines the fact that "on the 20th May 1453, the thousand year-old Byzantine Empire collapsed once and for all ... , followed by that accursed Lombard war that swallowed up military forces and money."[129] "Public debt had spiralled: emergency borrowing amounted to over fifty-nine percent of overall taxable property ... with dire consequences for the taxpayer."[130]According to Gino Luzzatto, "to avoid bankruptcy, Venice was obliged to deduct a third or more, often half of its citizens' incomes and also their manufacturing output, in tax."[131] Jean-Claude Hocquet asserts that "in Venice in 1471, with no end to the Turkish War in sight, utter destitution stalked the refugees driven from Romania for whom the Salt Office erected a covered shelter in the campo *San Antonio* to protect them from the cold, with the Grain Office handing out bread to them. In 1474, the Senate approved the conversion of this shelter into a permanent refuge for the poor ... 92 hospitals were created during the fourteenth and fifteenth centuries ... The influx of impoverished peasants into the city aroused dread since they could very well have come from areas where plague was rife with their confinement therefore justified on health grounds."[132] In Venice, vagabonds represented a "fully-fledged invasion force over six thousand strong "from a host of countries" .... And then there was the mass of beggars who were not all the genuine needy .... Finally there were the Jews ... , who had the run of the city, the cream of the crop of businessmen ... The State protected them from certain preachers' fanatical anti-Semitism, although this did not stop it from pressurizing their communities into making exorbitant loans"[133] observes an indignant Alvise Zorzi. On a more moderate note, Leon Poliakov makes the point that "at the time of the wars of the League of Cambrai [Venice having just lost the Terra ferma following defeat at the Battle of Agnadello in 1508], the Jews of Mestre and the *Terra ferma* sought refuge in Venice, as their *condotta* permitted in case of disturbances."[134]

By 1513 and 1514, Venice "was still beset by domestic problems that showed no sign of abating. There was plague in the city ... the Jews, scattered throughout the city, ... lent to the poor and to anyone else in financial trouble, and they had no shortage of clients."[135] When, in 1515, the Pregadi Council proposed to settle the Jews on the island of La Giudecca, "the Jewish community did not object to the principle but to the chosen location which they considered too dangerous"[136] on account of the group of mercenary militia stationed nearby, as Anne-Lise Polo explains. The representative of the Jewish community Anselmo del Banco suggested that they be sent to Murano. "The choice was a subtle one", notes Cecil Roth, "for the latter island was then reckoned the garden of Venice and was famous not only for its glass manufacture, but also for the sumptuous patrician villas latterly erected upon it ... the proposal was allowed to stand over."[137]

The debate resumed the following year. According to Riccardo Calimani, the Jews were accused of "numerous iniquities, including the illegal building of synagogues and corruption of the State."[138] In 1516, the Senate took "the decision to isolate the Jews within the city itself and to this end transfer them onto a small island in the parish of San Girolamo."[139] On the 29th March, a decree was enacted requiring "all the Jews to live together in the casserias [*corte de case*] which are in the Ghetto near San Girolamo"[140] in Calimani's first wording of it, morphing further on into " ... the Corte de Case situated at the Ghetto near San Girolamo."[141] On the 5th April, Anselmo del Banco tried again to object to the resolution, complaining that "the place designated was not large enough for the number of persons who would be forced to live there, which he estimated at 700. Many would be forced to leave the city"[142] after recently opening "their second-hand shops at Rialto and [making] heavy investments."[143] All of which was to no avail since, as Calimani points out, "the houses in the ghetto [were] evacuated immediately",[144] and "before the end of July, Asher Meshullam* (Anselmo del Banco) and his brother Chaim were forced to move into the ghetto. On moving to Venice, Chaim had imprudently rented the Ca' Bernardo palazzo in the parish of San Polo, ostentatiously flaunting his wealth and thereby arousing envy. The Meshullams were the heads of the wealthiest and most important banking family of Venetia."[145]

---

* Whose son became a Christian convert under the name of Marco Paradiso, as Elie Wiesel points out in his preface to Riccardo Calimani's The Ghetto of Venice. "Pope Clement VII himself came to the grandiose ceremony to offer his blessing".

The Jewish Ghetto

"For their being marked and distinct, as well as their dwellings as in their dress, is not so much due to the deprecation of the nations as it is the particular providence of their separation ..."
Isaac Cardoso, *Excellencies of the Hebrews* (1679)

"But for religion, and all the social rites and economic advantages that accompanied it, the wall would have turned the city into a prison, whose inmates would have had only one ambition: to destroy their keepers and break out."
Lewis Mumford, *The City In History*

a) Assignment

"The charter was about to expire and the usual precarious period of negotiation was beginning. In the summer of 1519, there was new talk of expulsion"[1] notes Riccardo Calimani, before the renewal of the Jews' residence permit was agreed upon, extending it this time to ten years "in exchange for a tax of ten thousand ducats, with the interest rate for loans set at 15 percent."[2] A series of hard-won charters eventually led the Jews to have their residence in the city legally recognized. Calimani describes "a unique period in the history of the Venetian Jews",[3] observing that "the fame of the Venetian ghetto spread to the most remote corners of the Diaspora."[4]

Stefano Zaggia asserts that on the 11th of June 1601 in Padua, "councillors backed a proposal put forward by the Jews to create a ghetto on a small island ("the island at the crossroads") … conforming to the needs of the community."[5] Two further proposals envisaged "the creation of a public space situated in the heart of the neighbourhood: "comprising a square surrounded by shops, within the said ghetto". The implication is immediately clear: the reference here is to what had become standard practice in the layout of the Ghetto Novo in Venice — the *corte de case* [the *corte de case* refers to the Arabic qaisariyya, a kind of agora or enclosed market: "There are also nine other Houses of note, which they call *Casseria's* or *Funduca's*"[6]] spread around a large square"[7] and which Donatella Calabi describes to us thus: "the zone was closed off by gates and bridges and partially surrounded by a canal which was patrolled by Christian guards. The houses were owned by Christian landlords and rented to the Jews (at a higher rate than for previous tenants), but were soon enlarged and transformed by their inhabitants, following the *jus gaz(z)agà*.[*] Jews added storeys to existing buildings, which they also subdivided intensively."[8]

Stefano Zaggia points out that "in Rovigo … on the 10th May 1627 … it had finally been decided to create

---

* *Combination of the Latin jus [law, right, justice, law court] and the Hebrew hazaqah "possession" (Umberto Fortis).*

an enclosed neighbourhood "forming a ghetto" by using walls and gates to separate a series of apartment buildings largely occupied by Jewish families, and especially by bankers, from the rest of the city",[9] noting that "the delays lengthened and decisions were postponed" owing to the fact that "when they first embarked on ghetto-building, the cities of Venetia did not have a ready-made fort like the ghetto of Venice at its disposal!"[10]

Leon Poliakov explains that in Rome, whose ghetto was modelled on the Venetian one, given that the houses "remained legally in the hands of their former Christian owners, ... to prevent speculation in rents, Pius IV included among the favours he did the Jews in 1562 an order that the amount charged should be controlled 'at a fair price', while the rabbis",[11] on the basis of the *jus gazagà*, guaranteed "that the Jews would permanently occupy their dwellings at extremely low rents"[12] with the result that "the statutory ghetto leases became ... one of the main factors in the wealth of its inhabitants, for the rich could speculate and invest their capital."[13] As in Venice, Poliakov draws attention to the fact that "the lack of space, the co-habitation of several tenants, or even families, in every room led to the creation of rights of way over entrances and corridors ... is sufficient to explain the staggering key-money of the *jus gazagà*."[14] Gérard Nahon makes the point that "the *hazaqah* prohibited all Jews, on pain of excommunication, from seeking to evict a Jewish tenant from his dwelling-place by offering a higher rent to the Christian owner .... The Jewish tenant thus enjoyed an unlimited *sitting tenancy*, i.e. a lease, that he could either sell, pass on to his heirs, or offer as a dowry to his daughter."[15]

To return to Venice, in a lecture given by Piero Falchetta at the Louvre Museum,[16] he explained that "the earliest realistic mapping of the city ... is also one of the chief masterpieces of urban cartography ever produced. In 1500 Jacopo de Barbari and the publisher Anton Kolb brought out their celebrated and peerless bird's-eye view of Venice, in which La Serenissima's seaboard outline and extraordinary architectonic otherness was accurately depicted for the first time."

José Lothe explains that "on the 30th of October 1500, Anton Kolb, a merchant from Nuremberg, had lodged a request with the Council of Venice for the right to distribute and export this map free of duty ... Kolb testified that three years work had been required to draw, engrave and print this map ... . Only a deep and applied knowledge of Euclidean geometry could have achieved such a level of accuracy in layout and depiction: all the evidence suggests that experienced Italian military engineers carried out the requisite measurements and calculations so that the topography, streets and buildings of all sizes could appear in such detail."[17] Indeed on close inspection, the group of houses that would later come to be known as the *Ghetto Novo* can clearly be made out on the Barbari map. It comprises a small, built-up island on which the houses are constructed level with the canals surrounding it, the houses themselves forming a walled enclosure and lending the whole the appearance of a fortress. Any suggestion that the area boasted an additional high wall is altogether fanciful since this function was already fulfilled by canals. Bernard Dov Cooperman confirms that "located as it was on the northern edge of the city, the *ghetto nuovo* ... contained no church or other sacred structure incompatible with the new purpose. Most especially to the point, the buildings there — a square constructed around a large central courtyard and in turn surrounded completely by water — already resembled a walled fortress."[18]

Highly conspicuous too is a recurrent and absolute

determination to depict the ghetto as some kind of prison, evidencing the morning opening and nightly closing of gates onto the bridges, to which one of the few retorts comes from Franco Filippi, pointing out that "the existence of three lending banks labelled red, *yellow and green** in the ghetto was no secret. It should be remembered that at that time and as is still the case today, the loans were made against pawned items and securities. It would therefore make perfect sense for those banks holding their customers' goods to take every precaution to guard against possible fires, thefts and robberies."[19] Thus the two gates "had to be opened in the morning and closed in the evening at sunset in accordance with the Hebrew calendar and timekeeping."[20] Élisabeth Crouzet-Pavan observes in addition that "in Venetian legislation, the whole issue of night increasingly took on manic proportions … Indeed night officially took place between the ringing of two secular bells: the first, *la Rialtina*, signalled lights out; the second, the morning *Marangona* in the campanile of St. Mark's, sounded the start of the working day."[21] Riccardo Calimani remarks that "like the Jews, the prostitutes were to begin their business only after the ringing of the Marangona."[22]

On the subject of the policing body of night watchmen to whom such importance is attached in order to reinforce this idea of imprisonment, Crouzet-Pavan's research sheds some light on their role in crime prevention. Thus, "in Venice … a city with no outer wall, … the watch seldom mounted a guard to look outwards. Here, the watch's focus was on the city and on the varying degrees and modes of domestic strife to which the night could give rise." However, pointing out a second peculiarity, she adds that, "just as was often the case in other urban

---

* *The colours of their overseers.*

settings, this surveillance was not confined to neighbourhood organizations or to guilds. It fell to public officials
... , Lords of the Night [*Domini de nocte*]."[23] In a further
observation, she concludes that "thefts under cover of
night were more specialized, systematic affairs — robberies committed in warehouses, communal granaries
or ships moored in the harbour. ... Ruled by merchant
patricians, the commercial city of Venice safeguarded her
economic system."[24]

As already noted, "confining foreigners was not
an exclusively Venetian custom. In Alexandria ... at night
they were locked in"[25] observes Riccardo Calmani, who
also draws attention to the fact that "the restrictions imposed on the Jews at that time must be viewed in the
overall context of the times. They were not the only group
or the only foreigners subject to such restrictions."[26]

Similarly, Robert Anchel notes that "during the
hours of dark at least, it was the common practice of
many cities in the Middle Ages to use gates to close off
some of their island precincts as a precaution against rob-
bers, a practice that had nothing ignominious about it."[27]

Roberta Curiel describes these points of ingress
and egress thus: "a small wooden bridge, rather like the
drawbridge of a medieval castle, and a narrow *sotopòrtego*
(a passageway through a building) connect the restricted,
secluded world of the Ghetto to the outside world. Holes
in the Istrian stone can easily be seen on either side of
the entrance to the *sotopòrtego*, in which were fixed the
hinges of one of the wooden gates which from 1516 to
1797 isolated the Jewish quarter from the rest of the city
at night."[28] There is the matter, however, of similar holes,
currently still visible or else clumsily daubed with ce-
ment in an effort to cover them up, that Curiel could not
be bothered to discover either side of the city's one hundred and sixty-seven *sottoportichi*.

In Stefano Zaggia's analysis, "within the urban fabric of Padua, of Verona and Rovigo, the location of the ghetto was in fact chosen according to the existence of a tacit containment zone that had long been occupied and structured by the Jewish community. In the last analysis, gating merely invests these areas with a physical boundary",[29] also pointing out "another interesting factor: Jewish communities betray a specific desire to equip these settlements with an organized, distributive network, not some zone cut off from the urban fabric, but a townlike, ordered and structured space, for Venice remained the model to be emulated … an open space where the houses, shops and amenities of the Jewish city overlooked a square; such appeared to be the "canonical" organization of that specific form of detached settlement called ghetto as contemporaries saw it."[30]

b) Occupancy

"The settlement of Jews in an outlying area of the city, well away from the main thoroughfares, caused a radical change in the ways of life of the various ethnic groups and in the structure of their host itself"[31] notes Umberto Fortis.

Leon Poliakov indicates that from the second half of the sixteenth century, "there were three communities of Jews at Venice: the 'Levantini' or oriental Jews; the 'Ponentini' or ex-Marranos (these two categories soon merged into one); and the community of Italian or Italo-German stock who were still designated as 'Tedeschi'."[32] The latter community hosted a sub-group of Ashkenazi German Jews who, since the end of the thirteenth century, had settled "in very many towns and villages throughout the north of Italy ... above all in Venetia ... . They formed the north-to-south influx that, along with the south-to-north trajectory of Roman Jews and with the less populous immigration from Savoy and Provence, contributed to the renewal of the Jewish presence in northern Italy",[33] as Alessandro Guetta outlines. The reason for this is furnished by Leon Poliakov: "while in southern bureaucratised Italy Judaism was in desperate straits, northern Italy, the Italy of the free towns, was opening up to it as a result of the money trade."[34]

Fernand Braudel argues that "these *Todeschi*, who had been accepted in the city at the time of the League of Cambrai, were poor Jews dealing in second-hand clothes and pawnbroking and they were to run the Monte di Pietà in Venice — *li banchi della povertà*";[35] whereas Umbert Fortis discloses that "the German "nation" was the only group to deal directly with the State, at least the only one cited in official documents"[36] probably after "the transformation of the lending banks into Banchi dei Poveri modelled on the Monti di Pietà set up in most of the other Italian towns to combat Jewish usury. ... the management and the financing of the *banchi*, till then administered by individuals, was made the responsibility of the "Tedeschi" community",[37] as Leon Poliakov has established.

Riccardo Calimani points out that "the residents of this city ... included many wayfaring Levantine Jewish merchants of Marrano origin, people of ambiguous religious affiliation. ... These merchants, Jews of Portuguese and Spanish origin, were called Levantine because they had lived in, or passed through, such eastern ports as Constantinople and Salonica before coming to Venice. Gradually they settled in the ghetto alongside the group of Jews called the German Nation, the core of the original community. ... There is no evidence of any instinctive empathy between the two Nations."[38] In addition, Calimani remarks that "the first group of Jews in the newly founded ghetto was called the "Natione Todesca", or German Nation ... Even at this time there were noticeable differences between Jews of German ancestry, accustomed to a hostile environment and themselves suspicious and unbending, and the Italian Jews who were reproached with ... being too indolent and "Mediterranean"."[39] Cecil Roth mentions that in Venice, "the Marranos had already begun to settle here at an early date, their expulsion being ordered by the scandalized Senate as far back as 1497. After the establishment of the Inquisition in Portugal, they began to turn their steps thither once again. Many of them went to join their coreligionists in the Ghetto. A greater number remained living among the ordinary population about the city, still wearing a transparent mask of Christianity, and proving strenuous competitors in trade."[40]

Umberto Fortis recounts that in 1541 "the small but rich group of Levantine Jews who had been confined in the New Ghetto since the start of the century — though never explicitly mentioned in the documents — and were by now well aware of their importance to the Venetian economy, applied to the senate for more suitable accommodation in the city, since the San Girolamo area was extremely restricted, already undeniably overcrowded, and therefore no longer adequate for the demands of all the commercial activity centering on the great trade with the east",[41] noting too that "subjects of the Turkish empire and foreigners in Venice ... the Senate's reply to the "wayfarers" [viandanti] (as the Levantine Jews were still called) was therefore positive, allowing these "separate" Jews, subject to other regulations and restrictions, to carry on their work and store their merchandise in the area adjoining the Ghetto Nuovo, the Ghetto Vecchio ... , an area ... very different in layout from the closed square of the Ghetto Nuovo":[42] "at that time the area comprised only a few houses and gardens"[43] in Roberta Curiel's stipulation. Riccardo Calimani comments that "in the Old Ghetto the Levantines had their warehouses and there were a few greengrocers and kosher butchers. ... of the estimated sixty thousand square meters available at that time, at least twenty-five thousand must have been shops and public facilities."[44]

Calimani explains too that "the edict of 1541 sanctioned the passing of Venetian trade, albeit only in part, from the hands of the Venetian patricians to those of the new foreign merchants",[45] observing elsewhere that ""the German Nation" lived in the New Ghetto and the Levantine Nation in the Old. Although they were neighbours, the two groups were now separate, and their functions in the economy were different."[46]

Roberta Curiel notes that "the Ghetto Nuovissimo ... was created in March 1633 to house the more privileged newcomers to the Ghetto ... , new families of Sephardic merchants ... . The Ghetto Nuovo and the Ghetto Vecchio were not overcrowded at the time, the plague of 1630-31 having claimed a large number of victims. ... The Ghetto Nuovissimo differed from the other two sectors of the Ghetto in not possessing the variety of little businesses which drew all sorts of different people to the area during the day, nor was there any of the life that took place around the synagogues ... so it was in practice simply a residential quarter for the wealthier Jews",[47] going on to describe "the most decent-looking building today ... is a twin *palazzo* with two elegant entrance porches ... . In the eighteenth century this was the residence of the dei Treves, one of the richest banking families in the history of the Venetian Ghetto ... . There are two double doors giving straight on to the canal to connect the palace directly with the outside world."[48]

Cecil Roth specifies that "the members of the new colony were known as "Ponentines" or Westerners; and in Venetian Jewry, they formed a distinct element by the side of the German and Levantine "nations" which already existed. ... Within a few years, they attained the hegemony in local affairs, in importance though not in numbers. They paid as much in communal taxation as the other two elements combined. In consequence, they were represented on the Council of the community by sixty members as against forty Germans ... and twelve Levantines",[49] moreover, "their synagogue, originally constructed in 1584 ... was the greatest and most luxurious in the Ghetto."[50]

c) Lines of business

Riccardo Calimani accepts that "we unfortunately know very little about the daily life of the ghetto during those early years, because the sources that have come down to us are primarily official documents, almost all relating to moneylending."[51] Nevertheless, Leon Poliakov reveals that "the *banchiere*, strong in his licence to settle, became a focus around whom gathered other Jews, his servants or small craftsmen. Then, if the colony prospered, they were joined by scholars and even artists."[52] Thus, "particularly in northern Italy, the *banchieri* were the pioneers of Jewish colonisation ... , once they had established themselves in a place, they helped co-religionists to settle there, if only to comply with the requirements of Jewish worship",[53] noting in particular that "the strict observance of Jewish religious ritual as guaranteed by the *condotta* required not only the services of a rabbi, a butcher for ritual slaughtering and a teacher ... but also the presence at daily prayers of a quorum (*minyan*) of ten Jewish men who had reached their religious majority. Thus ... [here] lies the explanation for the almost obligatory existence within the family circle of a *banchiere* of several other families, whatever their occupation, whose heads "did not bank"."[54]

Details of how the Banchi dei Poveri were run are provided by Leon Poliakov from an unpublished account: "The Monte is divided into three offices, each of which has its own colour ... . The office is on the ground floor of each of the houses which serve this purpose; these offices could be called shops, above which are the employees who keep the registers and value and receive securities; there, too, is the safe where gold and silver securities are shut away ... . The auction where the securities are sold is held at the Rialto."[55] If, as is suggested, "the administration of the Banchi dei Poveri, traditionally entrusted to certain ghetto families, should not have been a bad thing for them, it certainly was a bad thing for the Jewish community of Venice, which was responsible for supplying the working capital ... ." Poliakov then entertains the possibility that "the important Jewish businessmen who were the major support of the community found advantages in an insolvency which affected them not at all or only indirectly ... . Their wealth thenceforth came primarily from maritime trade."[56]

Giovanni Curatola mentions that even though "the business activities that they could undertake outside [the ghetto] were restricted",[57] "*strazzeria*, that is to say selling second-hand goods",[58] remained one of the statutes of the *condotta*. "The *mariegola*, or statutes, governing this latter activity — which was important, if limited — expressly mentioned that it could be performed by Jews; the statutes also list carpets among the goods permitted for re-sale."[59] To reiterate Curatola, "despite the loss of many documents on the role of Jewish merchants in Venetian trade, certain surviving evidence nevertheless indicates its importance."[60]

Referring to the historian Gino Luzzato, Leon Poliakov cites the following "minute from a Senate debate in 1541":[61] "the bulk of the merchandise which comes from upper and lower Romania is brought by, and found in, the hands of itinerant Levantine Jews",[62] just like "in the northern Adriatic, 'this trade is to a great extent in the hands of Jews'."[63] Fernand Braudel notes that "the regime introduced for 'Levantine' and 'Ponentine' Jews (*levantini* and *ponentini*) in 1598, was a genuinely liberal one: they were given passes valid for ten years which would automatically be renewed on expiry unless they were re-nounced."[64] Riccardo Calimani explains that "there was a significant change in Venetian trading policy: non-Venetian merchants were assured trading rights analogous to those reserved for the select Venetian merchant class. As Benjamin C. I. Ravid observed, this meant that the Western and Levantine Jews, most of whom were descended from Marranos, had rights to which more than 90 percent of the Venetian citizenry could not hope to aspire",[65] concluding that "Venice was at that time the most liberal port in Christian Europe for Jews and Marranos of every description."[66]

d) Community life

According to Alvise Zorzi, ""The University of the Jews" (meaning community), divided into three "nations", German, Levantine and Ponentine, was more prosperous and flourishing than most of the communities in the rest of Europe. It evolved under the benevolent gaze of the population which, according to Simone Luzzato, was kindlier and more obliging with the Jewish nation than any other people in the world."[67]

"In a sense", observes Umberto Fortis, "after the inevitable initial friction arising from never having experienced such cohabitation, the establishment of different groups in one place encouraged the gradual formation of a community spirit that transcended individuals ... [and] organizations and institutions able to meet the various demands of Jewish life",[68] in such a way that "its new circumstances led to the development of a typically Jewish rhythm of life, a rhythm of worship ... all revolving around the Sabbath."[69] "The ghetto" in Fernand Braudel's analysis, "may have been the prison within which the Jews were confined but it was also the citadel into which they withdrew to defend their faith and the continuity of the Talmud."[70] Similarly, Bernard Dov Cooperman notes that "the Ghetto's Jews did not refer to their enforced residence as a jail. Rather, it was the biblical 'camp of the Hebrews', a place of holiness while en route to the Promised Land ... Isaiah's Jerusalem ... and [Aboab's] choice of words tells us even more about how these Jews identified with their community-behind-walls and gloried in it."[71] In this connection, Edgar Morin mentions a Mosaic precept according to which "purists would not tolerate a gentile entering their homes."[72] As Umberto Fortis notes, "in short, the changes and innovations actually led to the building up of that unique and inimitable microcosm that the Jews themselves ... referred to as *hasèr*, the enclosed and isolated space that the Jewish spirit brought to life in a singular way."[73] According to Alan Unterman's definition, "*the eruv chatzerot* (mixed [ownership of] courtyards, domains) allows all the inhabitants of a given place (at block, street or even city-wide level) to be grouped together to form a single private sphere for the duration of the Shabbat ...the zone in question must be bounded by a real or symbolic wall."[74] "On the ground floor of the Spanish School", Thomas Jonglez and Paola Zoffoli point to the existence of "a curious map of Venice which shows the limits of the *eruv*";[75] adding "known as *eruv* ... , the Jewish community in Venice reached an agreement with the City Council. Via payment of a modest rent, various public areas alongside private properties were to be considered as belonging to the Jewish community as a whole."[76]

Such circumstances saw Venice become, as Fernand Braudel points out, "an intellectual capital. *Marrano* literature, both Spanish and Portuguese, was produced by Venetian printing presses, until their role was eventually taken over by the printers of Amsterdam and Hamburg."[77]

Frederic C. Lane notes that "both Jewish rabbis and Christian eulogists claimed that, after 1590, Jews were especially well treated in Venice. Christians went to concerts in the ghetto and Jews attended regattas and theatrical performances outside. They gambled together and listened to each other's sermons",[78] concluding that "Venice was considered a model republic when such models were very rare."[79]

Thus Roberta Curiel mentions that "the Rabbi Leon da Modena (1571-1648) was the leading figure during one of the most flourishing periods in the history of the Ghetto, a relatively stable period when exchanges between the cultural leaders of the Jewish quarter and Venetian intellectuals were particularly intense and productive. ... [his] sermons were attended by crowds of the nobility of Venice and even prelates of the church."[80] Similarly, "Sara Copio Sullam (1590?-1641), a friend of da Modena ... presided over a literary salon to which the brightest names in the Venetian cultural firmament used to come",[81] or "Leon da Modena's most brilliant disciple ... Simone Luzzato, author of a *Discourse on the State of the Jews*, published in 1638."[82] As Curiel further points out, at this time "Venice was one of the most important centres of Judaism in Europe, and rabbis and scholars from all over the world thought of this narrow quarter as an essential stopping-place on their peregrinations, and an essential part of their religious lives."[83] Writing in 1655, Menasseh ben Israel* had this to say: "In Italy [the Jews] are generally protected by all the Princes: their principall residence is the most famous City of Venice; so that in that same City alone they possesse about 1,400 Houses; and are used there with much courtesy and clemency."[84]

Riccardo Calimani has ventured that in this way, "the tiny ghetto grew to its final complex form, incorporating economic, cultural, social and religious aspects unique in their relationships with the Most Serene Republic of Venice and with the entire known world to the east and west."[85]

---

* *Menasseh ben Israel (1604-1657), a Dutch rabbi descended from Marranos.*

In Search of the Lost Ghetto

"Disputes about words are always disputes about things; for every man of honesty will confess, that he only uses this or that word from preference for this or that idea."
Madame de Staël, *Germany*

a) The quest

Nowadays it is accepted that the term *ghetto*, which was coined in Venice to denote the first residential quarter granted to the Jews by the Commune as the foregoing study has demonstrated, is *Venetian*. However, all manner of suggestions have been and are still being floated in order to endow it with a plausible etymology for want of a single clue about what it actually means.

It would therefore stand to reason to try and ascertain whether the word was understood from the outset with no pondering on the meaning necessary or whether this meaning came to elude the discernment of historians only at a later stage. A wealth of evidence would suggest, however, that these are the very two reasons why such a plethora of so-called etymologies, each one of which is as preposterous as the next, has come to prevail. When all that is known about a word with any certainty is its pronunciation, there is a tendency to look for some far-off or near equivalent that might shed some light on it among words that sound the same. An open season of sorts along semantic or phonetic lines, or even a combination of the two, is then declared that seeks to put a spin that may at the very least be described as eclectic on the whole exercise. Indeed the sheer range of suggestions in the following list illustrates this contention to a T.

The etymology given in Littré* has the word derive from the rabbinical Hebrew *ghet* [letter of divorce, repudiation] to which a rider from the Rabbi Samson Wertheimer was swiftly appended which runs thus: "Should a Hebraic origin be posited for the word, as its adoption in different languages would seem to warrant, then the only root words in this case could be ... 1) *Goudda-(h)*: separation, hedge, partition ... 2) *Ghetta*: flock, whose spelling is closer but whose meaning is slightly different. As far as the etymology *ghet* [letter of divorce] is concerned, it should be noted that this word does not mean separation ; it is in fact an abbreviation ... of the Latin *legatum*, ... the act of pointing out something to somebody. It is by no means certain that the word *ghetto* features in every language; but were this indeed to be the case here, nothing in particular would militate against the etymology from *borghetto* (diminutive in Italian of *borgo*, borough, district) given that the word and the thing have come to be intertwined the world over for my co-religionists of the Diaspora."

---

* *Émile Littré, Dictionnaire de la langue française.*

"Related, in the view of others, to the Syriac *Nghetto* which means congregation, synagogue", wrote Giuseppe Boerio in his *Dizionario del dialetto veneziano* (1856).

Among all the suggestions hazarded here and there post-Boerio, Umberto Fortis has, however, listed a variety of possible origins: in "German gehegt, meaning "enclosed" ... ; Old French gueat, meaning "guard" referring to the imposed supervisors ...; the Genoese getto, meaning "jetty, quay" where in 1492 the Jewish refugees from the Iberian peninsula were supposed to have been cast ("*gettati*") ... in Yiddish, earlier than the sixteenth century (Shmeruk*), and still others have thought of the German *Gitter* [grille], the Italian *borghetto* [borough, district], or the Old English gatwon ["street"] (Roth, etc.), but these are all barely reliable assumptions. The only certainty is that Venice not only wins the dubious prize for being the first to confine the Jews in an isolated enclosure, but enjoys the etymological distinction of having coined a term now used all over the world."[1]

Riccardo Calimani makes the case too that "the origin of the words *ghetto* and *giudecca* was a source of uncertainty for many illustrious scholars, Venetian and otherwise, including Muratori and Vettor Sandi. In our century, Benjamin C. I. Ravid has pointed out that the original documents establishing the ghetto in 1516 contain the spellings *geto* and *getto*, and that after 1541 we find *ghetto, gheto, geto* and *getto*. He therefore feels that the origin of the word is unclear and that any remaining doubts must concern the connection between *getto* and the verb *gettare**",[2] not without reason for herein lies the whole problem.

In 1992, an article was published on the subject by

* *Ex German Schmach? [affront, ignominy]!*
** *See below*

Benjamin C. I. Ravid entitled "From Geographical Realia to Historiographical Symbol: The Odyssey of the Word *Ghetto*"[3] where recourse is had to a variety of sources in order to ascertain the origin of a word indissociable from the Jewish settlement in Venice, "an event often completely shrouded in darkness or illuminated only by the dim light of dubious legend, [which] must be carefully examined."[4] While eventually conceding that "today it is generally presumed that the word derives from the Italian verb *gettare* (to pour or to cast), because of the previous presence of foundries in the area",[5] Ravid nevertheless points out that at the time of the joining of the *ghetto nuovissimo* to the two earlier ghettos (the *ghetto nuovo* (new) and the *ghetto vecchio* (old)), "this area was not designated by any name in the Senate legislation of 1633, but almost immediately it was being referred to by the Venetian authorities as the *ghetto nuovissimo*, i.e., the newest ghetto",[6] adding that "while the latter two designations had been in use prior to the residence of the Jews in those locations and apparently owed their origin to the former presence of foundries in the area, the ghetto nuovissimo had never been the site of a foundry"[7] and that the term had thus gone from an original specific usage (a foundry) to a generic usage (a segregated, walled-in Jewish quarter).

"The Jewish ghetto of Venice was apparently first mentioned in the Hebrew language in the *Diary* of David Ha-Reuveni, who came to Venice in the winter of 1523-24."[8] Ha-Reuveni explained to his readers that "the ghetto [is] the place of the Jews."[9] Similarly, Thomas Coryat's English-language *Coryat's Crudities* (London, 1611)* states that the author "was at a place where the whole fraternity

---

* *However, Cotgrave's Dictionarie of the French and English tongues of the same year contains no reference to it.*

of the Jews dwelleth together, which is called the Ghetto."[10] Benjamin C. I. Ravid goes on to note that "in later years, the Venetian origin of the word *ghetto* came to be forgotten ... and much ink was spilled by eighteenth-, nineteenth-, and twentieth-century authors in attempts to ascertain its etymology."[11] The article ends with the following observations: "to a great extent because of the negative connotations of the word *ghetto*, the nature of Jewish life in the ghetto is often misunderstood ... an extended investigation of why the word *ghetto* is used so loosely and imprecisely in Jewish history and contemporary sociology would reveal many complex motivations. The most common reason is no doubt merely a simple casual use of the word without any thought or awareness of its origin and nature. Others, however, are somewhat less innocent ... . Thus the word ghetto has become a value concept with negative connotations, rather than a descriptive word indicating a particular legal, residential system under which Jews lived."[12]

[For the reader's information, parallels could be drawn here with another "particular legal, residential system" known more topically as a "concession": "In Whampoa on the 24th October [1844], Théodore de Lagrené signed ... a thirty-six article treaty that laid a secure foundation for our trade relations with China ... ; for the purposes of our study, article 22 is of particular interest:
"All French nationals arriving in one of the five ports will, regardless of length of stay, be able to rent houses and goods depots ... set up churches, hospitals, hospices, schools and cemeteries. Following negotiations with the French consul to this end, the local authority will designate the most suitable quarters for the settlement of French nationals ... the Chinese authorities will prevent their own nationals from overpricing or imposing exorbitant tariffs, etc.".".[13]

Christine Cornet notes elsewhere that "from then on, these agreements would serve as a method of settling foreigners into legally self-governing enclaves",[14] drawing particular attention to the fact that "the plots of land ... were leased in perpetuity", yet remained "Chinese government property" whose "conventions were set down in a municipal document.[15]]

b) Inconsistencies

Although it could hardly be described as an early discovery, at first sight the etymology that has *ghetto* derive from a providential *geto* (in the sense of foundry) is not an unattractive one. However, it immediately begs several questions, and principally:

Why only after the Jewish settlement does this term *g(h)eto* make its appearance to denote a pre-existing quarter defined, as is customary in Venice, by its membership of a *contrada* (administrative subdivision) — in this instance that of San Girolamo in the *sestiere* (one of the six districts of Venice) of Cannaregio — , one moreover already built and inhabited (by Venetians) at the time of the transfer?

If it is the case that this zone was previously occupied by alleged *old, new,* and *newest* foundries, then why does no historian propounding this idea hazard even the slightest particular about these foundries' first appearance or the period of their working life? Indeed nothing seems to provide them with more copy than chatter about foundries for iron, copper or lead, not to mention the wherewithal for canons and mortars! This is of course when other pundits are not contending that this was in fact the place where these famed foundries were *pouring out or dumping* (Italian *gettare*) their slag (whence *getto*)! In that case, what name did the previous occupants of this accursed place (between hell and high water, it all depends) give to it? *Chi lo sa?*

There is nothing of course to rule out the existence in that area or elsewhere of the kind of small workshops where official or unofficial smelting went on at that time (as Martin Lowry recounts, "of the twelve printing presses in operation in1472 or before, nine of them had disappeared by 1474" following "suspicions that the circulation of counterfeit coins cast over printers as well as over tin and lead foundry workers"[16]), like the one that is still extant, hidden, near the Church of Madonna dell'Orto: "*The workshop of the Valese Iron Foundry* ... which still uses the best quality Fontainebleau sand ... a network of channels is created through which the molten metal flows ... and then sets to form the final shape";[17] or others, having been used to cast type. Frederic C. Lane contends that "even when supplemented with a font or two of type made from the punches, the equipment of a printer represented a capital investment hardly larger than the cost of paper for one book."[18]

[It should be borne in mind that print shops had been introduced into the Lagoon area as early as 1469 by John of Speyer and his brother Wendelin, followed by the German Christopher Waldarfer and the French printer Nicolas Jenson, and thereafter by compositors and engravers mainly from Germany. Indeed, over two hundred printing presses were in operation in the city (clustered around Rialto) right up to the end of the fifteenth century. Had these presses been grouped together and gradually spread across a number of areas along the same lines of development as the Venetian Arsenal, they would have left more of an impression on the collective memory. It should be noted accordingly that work to build the Arsenal started around 1104 (when the small island harbouring the ghetto was still marshland), and that, as Jean-Claude Hocquet characterizes it, "the Arsenal was a "war machine" where ... some craft shops specialized in arms manufacture ... others in artillery ... isolated behind its outer wall, it was a self-governing unit in which all State shipbuilding operations were clustered. It thus marks a radical departure from the scattered guild organization that had hitherto prevailed in the medieval urban world."[19]

Now for the attempt to extrapolate the designation *ghetto* from a presumed *foundry*. The Italian word for *foundry* is fonderia, and the Venetian is *fondaria*. In Venice, however, the separate term *getaria* "is used to denote a type foundry."[20] Whence *getto*, derived from *gettare* (meaning to throw, to pour — stones, water, etc., but also to cast molten metal); *far getto* means to cast in a mould, in other words to cast molten metal, hence *geto*, *getto* or *gitto* denoting a casting (whence the Venetian expression the *xe de geto*[21] which means that something is the spitting image of the original).

Gianfranco Siega observes that "the idea should be completely dismissed that the word *ghetto* derives from a supposed *ghetar* meaning to cast molten metal, which does not appear in Venetian and is certainly not Venetian (why the Germanic and unwarranted letter h that changes *geto* into *gheto*?)."[22] [Note that in Italian *g* is soft while *ghe/ghi* is hard].

Another kind of lumping together occurs in the case of the *getito* (ex Latin *gestum*) that appears in the charters concerning the ghetto and which is merely the "term used by the Venetian government to denote a duty or tax, a tax that each firm must pay on goods declared."[23]

Similarly, the term *getum* (merrily transformed into *ghettum*, in the same way that *getar* morphs into *ghetar*) then denoted the tax that funded public works such as the dredging of canals or the further development of the Venice Arsenal, and for which every resident landowner was liable. Umberto Fortis nevertheless sets out the plain facts of the matter: "[the Jews] were forced to run the ghetto pawnshops through their own bankers, and pay a heavy annual tribute (including 10,000 ducats for the Arsenal), the responsibility for collecting which fell on the community's administrative body."[24]

c) Closing remarks

Before reaching a conclusion, what lessons should be drawn from all the above? Firstly, that Venice was, for the West, both the initiator of and the heir to ancient traditions that turned it into a model commercial city. That this was underpinned by a set of economic and trade policies that were free from all outside interference; that it took preventative steps very early on to ensure that no one person could seize absolute power (as Donatella Calabi puts it: "the government of the dogeate is a constitutional republican system founded upon tight-knit affiliations, checks and balances",[25] or Alexandre Le Masson: "liable for every public office, displaying no favouritism, adding no title to their names, not recognizing any hierarchy within their ranks, the only privileges the patricians of Venice assumed were theirs as a matter of course were those of governing, devoting themselves to the service of the State, and being the head and the arm of the nation .... Everything for the people, nothing by the people was the motto of this aristocracy";[26] or Alvise Zorzi asserting that "there was no room for tyrants in Venetian civilization"[27]); and lastly, that in the best Byzantine tradition, it encouraged the residence of foreign merchants whose associations were supervised and safeguarded by the creation of appropriate magistracies. "Conscious of its peripheral nature, the Serene Republic always prized its reputation as a magnet, a compulsory stopping-off place, a transit port, and the crucial hub of its capital city's trade."[28] While defending its tacit interests, it seems that Venice adopted a firm yet noticeably benevolent approach towards all kinds of foreigner drawn not only by its prestige and wealth but also by the chance to ply a trade, indeed make money or, when all was said and done, live a better life there than anywhere else, anywhere else being those countries from which they were being driven by wars and expulsions. Otherwise, how can such an influx of people be explained?

Such was the context then in which Venice pioneered what has universally taken on the name of *ghetto*. The term would thenceforth serve to denote, particularly in Italy, a form of *concession* granted by a city to its Jewish community regardless of any other toponomastic consideration. This is why "called "New Egypt" by the Jews, [the *Judengasse* ("Jew's Lane")] was closed off by three gates which were open only during the hours of daylight. ... this was where the Jewish community lived, with all its institutions and all its trades and activities: moneydealers and peddlers; cattle-dealers and bankers; scholars, teachers, bakers, and art collectors; butchers, tailors, shoemakers; adults and children, the sick and the well. ... In this muddle of narrow-fronted houses, with rooms crammed in one beside another, one inside another, there developed a well-ordered, multifaceted, and intensive communal life ... In the sixteenth century it became famous far and wide through the work of its scholars ... [it] became the place where the *parnasim* (leaders of Jewish communities) from all over the Empire would assemble"[29] could very well be read as a description of the Venetian ghetto when in actual fact the place being described here is the Jewish quarter in Frankfurt am Main which predated the one in Venice by fifty years!

Simon Schwarzfuchs points, however, to another precedent: "the privilege accorded on the 13th September 1084 — the earliest for which we have any evidence — by Rudiger, Bishop of Speyer, to the city's Jews ... who decided to allow them in ... by surrounding their living quarters with a wall that would prevent the population from bothering them. The bishop undertook to procure the necessary plot of land by purchase, exchange or donation, the Jews undertaking for their part to pay him an annual fee in return ... . They would be authorized to exchange gold and money in their quarter, to buy and sell goods of every kind in the port and throughout the city. They would receive an additional plot of land to be used for the purpose of burying their dead",[30] etc. "This was not yet that period of the ghetto whose aim from the sixteenth century onward was to prohibit all contact between Jews and Christians",[31] is the same author's rather hasty conclusion.

For her part, Colette Estin deems it "common knowledge that the word ghetto has come to denote not only a circumscribed district in an administrative and coercive sense — as per the Italian "model" — , but also deliberate assembly within a separate quarter, a process that has been a feature of Jewish life from the earliest period of the Diaspora."[32]

On the other hand, Marion Kaminski points out

that "today the word *ghetto*, in the aftermath of the atrocities carried out by the Nazis, sends a shiver through all who hear it. What few people realize, however, is that this term was originally coined for the Jewish quarter of Venice and that for centuries it did not evoke terrible images but the exact opposite: the ghetto meant a guarantee of safety and protection."[33] In short, the complete reverse of the development that accompanied the term *Marrano* about which Cecil Roth writes that "it is the constancy shown by [the *Marranos*] and their descendants that has redeemed the term from its former insulting connotation, and endowed it with its enduring power of romance."[34]

Taken for granted over the long period of its usage, it would be reasonable to assume that each and every Venetian knew what the precise meaning of this term was, in exactly the same way that the term *fontego* would have been clear to them. This comparison, however, has nothing inadvertent about it.

It will be recalled that *fontego** (the Venetian form of the Italian fondaco) comes from the Arabic *al-funduq* or –*fondok* (synonym of *makzan*: storehouse, shop) denoting quarters or a building used as both a warehouse and an inn for foreign merchants on extended business trips to the Ports of the Levant, structures whose configuration and purpose were re-used by Venice for its architectural and urban programmes.** As we have also seen, similar forms and meanings of the same term acquired currency from around this period onward: *al-hondiga* [corn exchange] in Spain; while *al-fândega* took on the meaning of *customs house* in Portugal.

* Not to be confused with the Venetian fondago meaning the dregs of a liquid (wine, oil) at the bottom of a container.
** See chapter 3 (& note 44) supra for Wolfgang Kaiser's comparison between "fonduk" and ghetto in the division of urban space.

Countries that lie further away from Arabic-speaking regions have preserved the term *halle*,* the result by *apocope* (dropping of one or several syllables at the end of a word) of the Spanish *al-*(hondiga), or, by *aphaeresis* (dropping of phonemes at the beginning of a word), preserved *dok* (as in Dutch) from the original (al-fon) *dok* which survives in *dock*.** In the same way, the Portuguese (al-fan) *dega*, denoting customs house has given *Dogana*** (or *Doana* in Venetian), Venice's maritime customs house at the confluence of the Grand and the Giudecca Canals forming the famous *Punta della Dogana*.

To cite a better known example, it is common knowledge that the archaic term 'apothecary' comes from the Greek word *apothēkē* [storehouse], but from it too by aphaeresis come the Italian *bottega* [shop], the Spanish *bodega* [(wine) cellar, storeroom], and boutique. Or again that from the Arabic *(d)ārsinā'a* [house of art, industry, fabrication, construction] come *Arsenàl, Arsenale*, or *Arzanà***** in Venetian; but *darsena* [wet dock, open basin] in Genoese and *darse* [harbour, open basin, wet dock] in French.

Constantin François de Volney once noted that "by conveying the words of one language in the characters of another, they have so disfigured them as to render them difficult to be known ... . Any Arab, who should learn French, would not recognize in our maps

---

* *eg. French* halle *[(covered) market], cf. English* Hall, *the building of a guild: Fishmongers' Hall.*

** *Vast warehouse for maritime trade, where goods are stocked.*

*** *Or dock duties [French* octroi de mer]. *(The attempt to derive* octroi *from the French verb* octroyer *[to grant, give, bestow] is as silly as the effort to derive the French word* douane *[Customs (department)] from* Diwan, *the Ottoman Council Chamber).*

**** *Cf. "L'Arzanà de Veniziani" (Dante, Hell, Canto XXI).*

ten words of his own language."[35]

Let's return though to *Ghetto*.

Besides Venice's famous (German, Turkish, Persian) *fontegi* or residential inns, the name *fontego** (*fondaco* in Italian) was given to many warehouses or public and private shops. It should be reiterated that granaries were also called *fontigo*. As Jean-Claude Hocquet has pointed out: "millet was stocked next door to the *fondaco dei Turchi*, wheat at San Marco ... and at San Biagio near the Arsenal, flour at Rialto and San Marco. Stores of essential supplies were strategically located throughout the city in readiness for any eventuality."[36] Giuseppe Tassini similarly mentions a "*Fonteghetto Street at San Geremia*",[37] where a "*fonteghetto* (little *fondaco*) was situated ... probably one of the *Dominante's private Fonteghetti* against which different laws were promulgated between 1608 and 1706."[38]

Umberto Fortis provides us too with a chance piece of information when he refers to the likelihood of a banishment in 1496 of "Jewish groups from the old city centre to Mestre or other mainland towns, where a few surviving place-names such as *Piraghetto* in Mestre, the *Ghetto* district in Mogliano, *Via Giudecca* in Mirano, or *Via Ghetto* in Chirignago are indications of a former Jewish presence."[39] Unless of course former foundries are not to thank for them?

Giuseppe Tassini points out another example of false etymology on the subject of the *Campo delle Gatte* in Venice for which, according to successive land registry entries, popular tradition originally had the name *Campo de "legati* [apostolic nuncios], thereafter *deligati*, ending

---

* *Fondaco is explained thus in the Grande Dizionario Villanova italiano-francese of 1842: "Bottega, dove si vendono a ritagli panni e drappi" [draper's shop]; "magazzino per le vettovaglie" [supplies/ provisions outlet].*

up with *delle gate*, with each stage in the process bringing about a further corruption of the original name";[40] and which has nothing whatsoever to do with cats (*gatte* or *gate* in Venetian) even though they could still be found on the *campo* at that time.*

As in the case of *dock*, the term *Ghetto* is quite obviously just the end part of *fonteghetto* (*fondachetto*** in Italian), the diminutive of *fontego*, itself a term borrowed directly from the Arabic fonduk denoting a *caravanserai*-type concession reserved for a foreign community as a place of residence. Thus of all the possibilities suggested, Rabbi Samson Wertheimer's (see *supra*) was nearest the mark.

"There can be no doubt that, in the course of its development, historical research has gradually been led to place more and more confidence in the evidence of witnesses in spite of themselves"[41] was Marc Bloch's view. Might not the same be said of all research?

Venice-Paris, 2010-2011

---

* *Nowadays cats have been almost entirely eradicated from Venice. Dogs on leads are all that can be seen!*
** *Pronounced fon-da-kèt-to (Dizionario italiano-francese, Milano 1842) Translator's note*

Notes

The Foundations of the City

1   Nouma Fustel de Coulanges, *The Ancient City.*
2   Lewis Mumford, *The City in History.*
3   Auguste Jardé, *The Formation of the Greek People.*
4   Lewis Mumford, *op. cit.*
5   Auguste Jardé, *op. cit.*
6   Lewis Mumford, *op. cit.*
7   Bernard Lewis, *The Arabs in History.*
8   Lewis Mumford, *op. cit.*
9   Georges Jehel, *La Méditerranée médiévale* [The Mediterranean in the Middle Ages].
10   Émile Benveniste, *Le Vocabulaire des institutions indo-européennes* [Indo-European Institutional Vocabulary].
11   Lewis Mumford, *op. cit.*
12   Auguste Jardé, *op. cit.*
13   Gustave Glotz, *The Greek City.*
14   Auguste Jardé, *op. cit.*
15   Auguste Jardé, *op. cit.*
16   Auguste Jardé, *op. cit.*
17   Fustel de Coulanges, *op. cit.*
18   Pierre Roussel, *La Grèce et l'Orient, des guerres médiques à la conquête romaine* [Greece and the Orient, from the Medic Wars to the Roman Conquest].
19   Auguste Jardé, *op. cit.*
20   Lewis Mumford, *op. cit*
21   Pierre Roussel, *op. cit.*

22   Lewis Mumford, *op. cit.*

23   Gustave Glotz, *op. cit.*

24   Lewis Mumford, *op. cit.*

The Cosmopolitan City

1   Ferdinand Lot, *The End of the Ancient World and the Beginning of the Middle Ages.*

2   Pierre Roussel, *op. cit.*

3   *Ibidem.*

4   Lewis Mumford, *op. cit.*

5   Charles Diehl, *Histoire de l'Empire byzantin* [History of the Byzantine Empire].

6   *Ibidem.*

7   *Ibidem.*

8   *Ibidem.*

9   *Ibidem.*

10   Alvise Zorzi, *History of Venice.*

11   *Ibidem.*

12   *Ibidem.*

13   Élisabeth Crouzet-Pavan, *Venice Triumphant.*

14   Frederic C. Lane, *Venice A Maritime Republic.*

15   Frederic C. Lane, *op. cit.*

16   Jean Longnon, *L'Empire latin de Constantinople* [The Latin Empire of Constantinople].

17   Freddy Thiriet, *Histoire de Venise* [History of Venice].

18   *Ibidem.*

19   Charles Diehl, *op. cit.*

20   Pierre Roussel, *op. cit.*

21   Bernard Lewis, *op. cit.*

22   Abram Leon, *The Materialist Conception of the Jewish Question.*

23   Gianluigi Barni, *La Conquête de l'Italie par les Lom-*

bards [The Lombard Conquest of Italy].

24   Jean-Claude Hocquet, *Venise au Moyen Âge* [Venice in the Middle Ages].

25   Frederic C. Lane, *op. cit.*

26   *Ibidem.*

27   *in Dictionnaire du Moyen Âge* [Dictionary of the Middle Ages] (Presses Universitaires de France).

28   Anne Raulin, *Anthropologie urbaine* [Urban Anthropology].

29   Jean de Joinville, *History of Saint Louis.*

30   De Breves, *Voyage en Turquie* [Journey to Turkey

31   Jean-Claude Hocquet, *op. cit.*

32   Frederic C. Lane, *op. cit.*

33   *Ibidem.*

34   *Ibidem.*

35   *Ibidem.*

36   *Ibidem.*

37   Philippe Braunstein and Robert Delort, *Venise, portrait historique d'une ville* [Historical Portrait of the City of Venice].

38   Paul Morand, *Venise sur la route des Indes* [Venice Indies Bound].

39   Alvise Zorzi, *op. cit*

40   Jean-Claude Hocquet, *op. cit.*

41   Philippe Braunstein and Robert Delort, *op. cit.*

42   Frederic C. Lane, *op. cit.*

43   Christian Bec, *Histoire de Venise* [History of Venice].

44   Alvise Zorzi, *op. cit.*

45   Frederic C. Lane, *op. cit.*

46   *Ibidem.*

47   *Ibidem.*

48   Alvise Zorzi, *op. cit.*

The Jewish Community: Exile to Exile.

1   Shlomo Sand, *The Invention of the Jewish People.*

2   *Ibidem.*

3   *Ibidem.*

4   Simon Schwarzfuchs, *Kahal, la communauté juive de l'Europe médiévale* [Kahal, the Jewish Community of Medieval Europe].

5   Leon Poliakov, *Jewish Bankers and the Holy See from the Thirteenth to the Seventeenth Centuries.*

6   Shlomo Sand, *op. cit.*

7   *Ibidem.*

8   *Ibidem.*

9   *Ibidem.*

10   *Ibidem.*

11   *Ibidem.*

12   Theodor Mommsen, *The History of Rome.*

13   *Ibidem.*

14   Simon Schwarzfuchs, in *Mille Ans de cultures ashkénazes* [One Thousand Years of Ashkenazi Cultures].

15   Simon Schwarzfuchs, Kahal ... *op. cit.*

16   Abram Leon,*op. cit.*

17   Simon Schwarzfuchs, *op. cit.*

18   Introduction to *One Thousand Years of Ashkenazi Cultures, op. cit.*

19   Abram Leon, *op. cit.*

20   *Ibidem.*

21   *Ibidem.*

22   Nachum T. Gidal, *Jews in Germany from Roman Times to the Weimar Republic*

23   Abram Leon, *op. cit.*

24   Marc Bloch, *Feudal Society.*

25   Aron J. Gurevich, *The Merchant in "The Medieval World",* edited by Jacques Le Goff.

26   Nachum T. Gidal, *op. cit.*

27   Aron J. Gurevich, *op. cit.*

28   *Ibidem.*

29   Nachum T. Gidal, *op. cit*

30   Sylvie Anne Goldberg, in *One Thousand Years of Ashkenazi Cultures, op. cit.*

31   Introduction to One Thousand Years of Ashkenazi Cultures, *op. cit.*

32   Riccardo Calimani, *L'Errance juive* [Jewish Wanderings].

33   Israel Bartal, *L'Implantation des Ashkénazes en Europe de l'Est* [Ashkenazi Settlement in Eastern Europe] in *A Thousand Years ... op. cit.*

34   Robert Anchel, *Les Juifs en France* [The Jews in France].

35   Simon Schwarzfuchs, *op. cit*

36   *Ibidem.*

37   *Ibidem.*

38   Stefano Zaggia, *Contrade juives et ghettos* [Jewish contrade and ghettos] in *Les Étrangers dans la ville* [Foreigners in the City].

39   Robert Anchel, *op. cit.*

40   *Ibidem.*

41   *Ibidem.*

42   Fernand Braudel, *The Mediterranean and the Mediterranean World in the Age of Philip II.*

43   Leon Poliakov, *op. cit.*

44   Wolfgang Kaiser, *Récits d'espace* [Spatial Tales] in Foreigners in the City, *op. cit.*

45   Sylvie Anne Goldberg, *op. cit.*

46   *Ibidem.*

47   in *Dictionnaire encyclopédique du judaïsme* [Encyclopedia of Judaism] (éditions Laffont).

48   Alan Unterman, *Dictionnaire du judaïsme* [Dictionary of Judaism].

49   Simon Schwarzfuchs, *op. cit.*

50   Abram Leon, *op. cit.*

51   *Ibidem.*

52   *Ibidem.*

53   *Ibidem.*

54   *Ibidem.*

55   Wolfgang Kaiser, *op. cit.*

56   Michael Wex, *Born to Kvetch.*

57   *Ibidem.*

58   *Ibidem.*

59   Simon Schwarzfuchs, in *One Thousand Years of Ashkenazi Cultures.*

60   *Ibidem.*

61   Béatrice Philippe, *Être juif dans la société française* [Being Jewish in French Society].

62   *Ibidem.*

63   *Ibidem.*

64   Gilbert Dahan, in *One Thousand Years ... op. cit.*

65   *Ibidem.*

66   *Ibidem.*

67   *Ibidem.*

68   Riccardo Calimani, *op. cit.*

69   Sylvie Anne Goldberg, *op. cit.*

70   Riccardo Calimani, *op. cit.*

71   Gilbert Dahan, *op. cit.*

72   Henry Charles Lea, *History of the Inquisition in the Middle Ages.*

73   *Ibidem.*

74   *Ibidem.*

75   Simon Schwarzfuchs, Kahal ... , *op. cit.*

76   *Ibidem*

77   Henry Charles Lea, *op. cit.*

78   *Ibidem.*

79   Béatrice Leroy, *Les Juifs dans l'Espagne chrétienne avant 1492* [The Jews in pre-1492 Christian Spain].

80   *Ibidem.*
81   Henry Charles Lea, *op. cit.*
82   Gilbert Dahan, *op. cit*
83   *Ibidem.*
84   Abram Leon, *op. cit*
85   *Ibidem.*
86   *Ibidem.*
87   *Ibidem.*
88   *Ibidem.*
89   Fernand Braudel, *op. cit.*
90   Cecil Roth, *History of the Marranos.*
91   Shlomo Sand, *op. cit.*
92   Béatrice Leroy, *op. cit.*
93   *Ibidem.*
94   Cecil Roth, *op. cit.*
95   Jean Descola, *A History of Spain.*
96   Cecil Roth, *op. cit.*
97   Jean Descola, *op. cit*
98   *Ibidem.*
99   Bernard Lewis, *The Jews of Islam.*
100   Joseph Calmette, *L'Élaboration du monde moderne*
[The Development of the Modern World].
101   Bernard Lewis, *op. cit.*
102   *Ibidem.*
103   Alexandre Skirda, *La Traite des Slaves* [The Slav
Trade].
104   Bernard Lewis, *op. cit.*
105   *Ibidem.*
106   *Ibidem.*
107   *Ibidem.*
108   *Ibidem.*
109   Charles E. Dufourcq, *La Vie quotidienne dans
l'Espagne médiévale sous domination arabe* [Daily Life in
Medieval Spain under Arab Rule].
110   Shlomo Sand, *op. cit.*

111   *Ibidem.*

112   *Ibidem.*

113   Cecil Roth, *op. cit.*

114   *Ibidem.*

115   Jean-Pierre Dedieu, *Le Reflux de l'Islam espagnol* [The Ebb of Spanish Islam].

116   Jean Descola, *op. cit.*

117   Bartolomé Bennassar, *L'Inquisition espagnole* [The Spanish Inquisition].

118   Jean-Pierre Dedieu, *op. cit.*

119   *Ibidem.*

120   *Ibidem.*

121   *Ibidem.*

122   Louis Cardaillac, *Pour clocher un minaret* [Minaret for Steeple].

123   Jean-Pierre Dedieu, *op. cit.*

124   *Ibidem.*

125   *Ibidem.*

126   *Ibidem.*

127   *Ibidem.*

128   *Ibidem.*

129   Bartolomé Bennassar, *op. cit.*

130   Yosef Hayim Yerushalmi, *From Spanish Court to Italian Ghetto.*

131   *Ibidem.*

132   *Ibidem.*

133   Esther Benbassa and Aron Rodrigue, *Sephardi Jewry.*

134   *Ibidem.*

135   Riccardo Calimani, *op. cit.*

136   *Ibidem.*

137   *Ibidem.*

138   *Ibidem.*

139   *Ibidem.*

140   Pilar León Tello, *La Juderia, un air de réussite* [Jew-

ry On the Up].

141   Esther Benbassa and Aron Rodrigue, *op. cit.*

142   Bartolomé Bennassar, *op. cit.*

143   *Ibidem.*

144   Pilar León Tello, *op. cit.*

145   Riccardo Calimani, *op. cit.*

146   *Ibidem.*

147   Pilar León Tello, *op. cit.*

148   Henry Charles Lea, *op. cit.*

149   *Ibidem.*

150   *Ibidem.*

151   Esther Benbassa and Aron Rodrigue, *op. cit.*

152   Henry Charles Lea, *op. cit.*

153   Cecil Roth, *op. cit.*

154   Bartolomé Bennassar, *op. cit.*

155   Riccardo Calimani, *op. cit.*

156   *Ibidem.*

157   *Ibidem.*

158   *Ibidem.*

159   Bartolomé Bennassar, *op. cit.*

160   *Ibidem.*

161   Cecil Roth, *op. cit.*

162   *Ibidem.*

163   *Ibidem.*

164   Riccardo Calimani, *op. cit.*

165   Bartolomé Bennassar, *op. cit.*

166   *Ibidem.*

167   *Ibidem.*

168   Jaime Contreras, *Pouvoir et Inquisition en Espagne au XVIème siècle* [Authority and Inquisition in Sixteenth Century Spain].

169   Esther Benbassa and Aron Rodrigue, *op. cit.*

170   Isidoro La Lumia, *Histoire de l'expulsion des Juifs de Sicile* [History of the Eviction of the Jews from Sicily].

171   Esther Benbassa and Aron Rodrigue, *op. cit.*

172 Jean Descola, *op. cit.*
173 *Ibidem.*
174 *Ibidem.*
175 Bartolomé Bennassar, *op. cit.*
176 Cecil Roth, *op. cit.*
177 Bernard Lewis, *op cit.*
178 Riccardo Calimani, *op. cit.*
179 Cecil Roth, *op. cit.*
180 In Miguel A. Arias de la Cruz, *Americanismos* (Editorial Everest).
181 Cecil Roth, *op. cit.*
182 *Ibidem.*
183 *Ibidem.*
184 Béatrice Leroy, *op. cit*
185 *Ibidem.*
186 Cecil Roth, *op. cit.*
187 *Ibidem.*
188 *Ibidem.*
189 Yosef Hayim Yerushalmi, *op. cit.*
190 Anne-Lise Polo, *La Nef marrane* [The Marrano Ship].
191 Riccardo Calimani, *op. cit.*
192 Cecil Roth, *op. cit.*
193 Yosef Hayim Yerushalmi, *op. cit.*
194 *Ibidem.*
195 *Ibidem.*
196 *Ibidem.*
197 Riccardo Calimani, *op. cit.*
198 *Ibidem.*
199 Cecil Roth, *op. cit.*

Venice, a City State

1   Jean-Claude Hocquet, *op. cit.*
2   Freddy Thiriet, *op. cit.*
3   *Ibidem.*
4   Frederic C. Lane, *op. cit*
5   *Ibidem.*
6   *Ibidem.*
7   Egle Trincinato in *Venise au fil du temps* [Venice Down Through the Ages] (*Atlas historique d'urbanisme et d'architecture* [Historical Atlas of Urbanism and Architecture]).
8   Philippe Braunstein and Robert Delort, *op. cit.*
9   Frederic C. Lane, *op. cit.*
10   Christian Bec, *op. cit.*
11   Élisabeth Crouzet-Pavan, *op. cit*
12   *Ibidem.*
13   *Ibidem.*
14   Jean-Claude Hocquet, *op. cit.*
15   *Ibidem.*
16   *Ibidem.*
17   *Ibidem.*
18   *Ibidem.*
19   Pierre Moukarzel, *Les Marchands européens dans l'espace urbain mamelouk* (*Colloque sur le thème des Minorités et régulations sociales en Méditerranée médiévale*) [European Merchants in Mameluk Cities — Conference on Minorities and Social Control in the Medieval Mediterranean].
20   *Ibidem.*
21   *Ibidem.*
22   *Ibidem.*
23   Donatella Calabi, *Venise au fil de son histoire* [Venice Down Through Its History].

24   Franco Filippi, *Anche questa è Venezia* [All Venice and More].

25   Marie F. Viallon, *Venise et la Porte ottomane 1453-1566* [Venice and the Ottoman Porte].

26   Donatella Calabi, *op. cit.*

27   Frederic C. Lane, *op. cit.*

28   Lewis Mumford, *op. cit.*

29   Frederic C. Lane, *op. cit.*

30   Marie F. Viallon, *op. cit.*

31   *Ibidem.*

32   Lewis Mumford, *op. cit.*

33   *Ibidem.*

34   Philippe Braunstein and Robert Delort, *op. cit.*

35   Bernard Doumerc, *Des Échelles du Levant aux brumes atlantiques* [From the Ports of the Levant to Atlantic Mists] *in série Mémoires no. 22* (éditions Autrement).

36   *Ibidem.*

37   *Ibidem.*

38   Jean-Claude Hocquet, *op. cit.*

39   *Ibidem.*

40   Frederic C. Lane, *op. cit.*

41   *Ibidem.*

42   *Ibidem.*

43   *Ibidem.*

44   Jean-Claude Hocquet, *op. cit.*

45   *Ibidem.*

46   *Ibidem.*

47   Reinhold Mueller, *Les étrangers naturalisés à Venise entre les XIVe et XVIe siècles* [Naturalized Foreigners in Venice from the Fourteenth to the Sixteenth Centuries] in *Foreigners in the City, op. cit.*

48   Jean-Claude Hocquet, *op. cit.*

49   *Ibidem.*

50   *Ibidem.*

51   Élisabeth Crouzet-Pavan, *op. cit.*

52   Donatella Calabi, *op. cit.*
53   Philippe Braunstein and Robert Delort, *op. cit.*
54   *Ibidem.*
55   Alvise Zorzi, *op. cit*
56   *Ibidem.*
57   Donatella Calabi, *op. cit.*
58   Venice Down Through the Ages, *op. cit.*
59   Anne Raulin, *op. cit.*
60   Bernard Doumerc, *op. cit.*
61   Élisabeth Crouzet-Pavan, *op. cit.*
62   René Guerdan, *La Sérénissime* [The Serenissima].
63   Donatella Calabi, *op. cit.*
64   *Ibidem.*
65   Julian Raby, *The Serenissima and the Sublime Porte: Art in the Art of Diplomacy 1453-1600* in *"Venice and the Islamic World 828-1797"* (New York-New Haven-London).
66   Frederic C. Lane, *op. cit.*
67   Giuseppe Tassini, *Curiosità veneziane* [Venetian Curiosities].
68   Jean-François Chauvard, *Échelles d'observation et insertion des étrangers dans l'espace vénitien* [Observation Ladders and Foreigner Inclusion in Venice] in *Foreigners in the City, op. cit.*
69   *Ibidem.*
70   *Ibidem.*
71   Donatella Calabi, *op. cit.*
72   *Ibidem.*
73   Frederic C. Lane, *op. cit.*
74   *Ibidem.*
75   *Ibidem.*
76   Henry Charles Lea, *op. cit*
77   *Ibidem.*
78   *Ibidem.*
79   *Ibidem.*
80   *Ibidem.*

81   *Ibidem.*
82   Frederic C. Lane, *op. cit.*
83   *Ibidem.*
84   Marie F. Viallon, *op. cit.*
85   *Ibidem.*
86   Riccardo Calimani, *op. cit.*
87   Frederic C. Lane, *op. cit.*
88   *Ibidem.*
89   Franco Filippi, *op. cit*
90   Élisabeth Crouzet-Pavan, *Venise une invention de la ville* [Venice: Devising the City].
91   *Ibidem.*
92   *Ibidem.*
93   *Ibidem.*
94   Frederic C. Lane, *op. cit.*
95   Élisabeth Crouzet-Pavan, *op. cit.*
96   Aron J. Gurevich, *op. cit.*
97   *Ibidem.*
98   Leon Poliakov, *op. cit.*
99   Quoted in Leon Poliakov, *op. cit.*
100 Aron J. Gurevich, *op. cit.*
101 *Ibidem.*
102 Leon Poliakov, *op. cit.*
103 *Ibidem.*
104 *Ibidem.*
105 Jean-Claude Hocquet, *op. cit.*
106 Leon Poliakov, *op. cit.*
107 *Ibidem.*
108 Cecil Roth, *Venice* (The Jewish Publication Society of America).
109 Jean-Claude Hocquet, *op. cit.*
110 Riccardo Calimani, *The Ghetto of Venice.*
111 Roberta Curiel, A Tour of the Ghetto, in *"The Ghetto of Venice"*.
112 Riccardo Calimani, *op. cit.*

113   *Ibidem.*
114   *Ibidem.*
115   *Ibidem.*
116   *Ibidem.*
117   Roberta Curiel, *op. cit.*
118   Riccardo Calimani, *op. cit.*
119   *Ibidem.*
120   *Ibidem.*
121   *Ibidem.*
122   *Ibidem.*
123   *Ibidem.*
124   *Ibidem.*
125   Giovanni Curatola, *Ebrei, Turchi e Veneziani a Rialto* [Jews, Muslims and Venetians at Rialto].
126   Giovanni Curatola, *Venice's Textile and Carpet Trade: The Role of Jewish Merchants in "Venice and the Islamic World 828-1797", op. cit.*
127   Riccardo Calimani, *op. cit.*
128   *Ibidem.*
129   Alvise Zorzi, *op. cit.*
130   *Ibidem.*
131   Quoted in Alvise Zorzi, *op. cit.*
132   Jean-Claude Hocquet, *op. cit.*
133   Alvise Zorzi, *op. cit.*
134   Leon Poliakov, *op. cit.*
135   Riccardo Calimani, *op. cit.*
136   Anne-Lise Polo, *op. cit.*
137   Cecil Roth, *History of the Jews in Venice.*
138   Riccardo Calimani, *op. cit.*
139   *Ibidem.*
140   *Ibidem.*
141   *Ibidem.*
142   Cecil Roth, *op. cit.*
143   Riccardo Calimani, *op. cit.*
144   *Ibidem.*

145   *Ibidem.*

The Jewish Ghetto

1   Riccardo Calimani, *op. cit.*
2   *Ibidem.*
3   *Ibidem.*
4   *Ibidem.*
5   Stefano Zaggia, *op. cit*
6   Olfert Dapper, *Description of Africa*, 1670 (trans. John Ogilby).
7   Stefano Zaggia, *op. cit.*
8   Donatella Calabi, *Foreigners and the City: An Historiographical Exploration of the Early Modern Period.*
9   Stefano Zaggia, *op. cit.*
10   *Ibidem.*
11   Leon Poliakov, *op. cit.*
12   *Ibidem.*
13   *Ibidem.*
14   *Ibidem.*
15   Gérard Nahon, *in Encyclopaedia Universalis, article entitled Ghetto.*
16   in November 1996.
17   José Lothe, *Initiation à l'histoire de la gravure [Introduction to the History of Engraving] (Annuaire de l'EPHE).*
18   Bernard Dov Cooperman, in Roberta Curiel, *"The Ghetto of Venice", op. cit. (Introduction).*
19   Franco Filippi, *op. cit.*
20   *Ibidem.*
21   Élisabeth Crouzet-Pavan, *op. cit.*
22   Riccardo Calimani, *op. cit.*
23   Élisabeth Crouzet-Pavan, *op. cit.*
24   *Ibidem.*

25   Riccardo Calimani, *op. cit.*

26   *Ibidem.*

27   Robert Anchel, *op. cit.*

28   Roberta Curiel, *op. cit.*

29   Stefano Zaggia, *op. cit.*

30   *Ibidem.*

31   Umberto Fortis, *The Ghetto on the Lagoon.*

32   Leon Poliakov, *op. cit.*

33   Alessandro Guetta, *Les Juifs ashkénazes en Italie* [*Ashkenazi Jews in Italy*] in One Thousand Years of Ashkenazi Cultures, op. cit.

34   Leon Poliakov, *op. cit.*

35   Fernand Braudel, *op. cit.*

36   Umberto Fortis, *op. cit.*

37   Leon Poliakov, *op. cit.*

38   Riccardo Calimani, *op. cit.*

39   *Ibidem.*

40   Cecil Roth, History of the Marranos, *op. cit.*

41   Umberto Fortis, *op. cit.*

42   *Ibidem.*

43   Roberta Curiel, *op. cit.*

44   Riccardo Calimani, *op. cit.*

45   *Ibidem.*

46   *Ibidem.*

47   Roberta Curiel, *op. cit.*

48   *Ibidem.*

49   Cecil Roth, op. cit.

50   *Ibidem.*

51   Riccardo Calimani, *op. cit.*

52   Leon Poliakov, *op. cit.*

53   *Ibidem.*

54   *Ibidem.*

55   *Ibidem.*

56   *Ibidem.*

57   Giovanni Curatola, *Tissus et tapis à Venise, le rôle*

des marchands juifs dans leur commerce [The Role of Jewish Merchants in the Textile and Carpet Trade in Venice].

58   *Ibidem.*

59   *Ibidem.*

60   *Ibidem.*

61   Leon Poliakov, *op. cit.*

62   *Ibidem.*

63   *Ibidem.*

64   Fernand Braudel, *op. cit.*

65   Riccardo Calimani, *op. cit.*

66   *Ibidem.*

67   Alvise Zorzi, *op. cit.*

68   Umberto Fortis, *op. cit.*

69   *Ibidem.*

70   Fernand Braudel, *op. cit.*

71   Bernard Dov Cooperman, *op. cit.*

72   Edgar Morin, *Vidal and His Family: From Salonica to Paris: the Story of a Sephardic Family in the Twentieth Century.*

73   Umberto Fortis, *op. cit.*

74   Alan Unterman, *op. cit.*

75   Thomas Jonglez and Paola Zoffoli, *Secret Venice.*

76   *Ibidem.*

77   Fernand Braudel, *op. cit.*

78   Frederic C. Lane, *op. cit.*

79   *Ibidem.*

80   Roberta Curiel, *op. cit.*

81   *Ibidem.*

82   *Ibidem.*

83   *Ibidem.*

84   Menasseh ben Israel, *Humble Address to His Highnesse the Lord Protector of the Common-Wealth of England, Scotland and Ireland.*

85   Riccardo Calimani, *op. cit.*

In Search of the Lost Ghetto

1   Umberto Fortis, *op. cit.*
2   Riccardo Calimani, *op. cit*
3   Benjamin C. I. Ravid, *From Geographical Realia to Historiographical Symbol: The Odyssey of the Word Ghetto* (in "Essential Papers on Jewish Culture in Renaissance and Baroque Italy", edited by David B. Ruderman, New York University Press, New York & London).
4   *Ibidem.*
5   *Ibidem.*
6   *Ibidem.*
7   *Ibidem.*
8   *Ibidem.*
9   *Ibidem.*
10   *Ibidem.*
11   *Ibidem.*
12   *Ibidem.*
13   Charles B.-Maybon and Jean Fredet, *Histoire de la Concession française de Changhaï* [History of the French Concession in Shanghai].
14   Christine Cornet, *Shanghaï avant Shanghaï* [Shanghai before Shanghai].
15   *Ibidem.*
16   Martin Lowry, *L'imprimerie, un nouveau produit culturel* [Printing: A New Cultural Product] in "*Venise 1500*" (éditions Autrement).
17   Thomas Jonglez and Paola Zoffoli, *op. cit.*
18   Frederic C. Lane, *op. cit.*
19   Jean-Claude Hocquet, *op. cit.*
20   Giuseppe Boerio, *Dizionario del dialetto veneziano, op. cit.*
21   *Ibidem.*
22   Gianfranco Siega, *Il Dialetto perduto* [The Lost

Dialect].

23   Giuseppe Boerio, *op. cit.*

24   Umberto Fortis, *op. cit.*

25   Donatella Calabi, *op. cit.*

26   Alexandre Le Masson, *Venise en 1848 et 1849* [Venice in 1848 and 1849].

27   Alvise Zorzi, *op. cit.*

28   Donatella Calabi, *op. cit.*

29   Nachum T. Gidal, *op. cit.*

30   Simon Schwarzfuchs, *op. cit.*

31   *Ibidem*.

32   Colette Estin, *L'Apartheid des temps modernes* [The Apartheid of Modern Times] (*in Notre Histoire*, no 16).

33   Marion Kaminski, *Venice, Art and Architecture.*

34   Cecil Roth, *op. cit.*

35   Constantin François de Volney, *Travels Through Syria and Egypt in the Years 1783, 1784 and 1785.*

36   Jean-Claude Hocquet, *op. cit.*

37   Giuseppe Tassini, *op. cit.*

38   *Ibidem*

39   Umberto Fortis, *op. cit.*

40   Giuseppe Tassini, *op. cit.*

41   Marc Bloch, *The Historian's Craft.*